Joseph James Gormully, Robert Victor Sinclair

Banks and Banking

Containing a full Annotation of 'The Bank Act'. Second Edition

Joseph James Gormully, Robert Victor Sinclair

Banks and Banking
Containing a full Annotation of 'The Bank Act'. Second Edition

ISBN/EAN: 9783337108366

Printed in Europe, USA, Canada, Australia, Japan

Cover: Foto ©Suzi / pixelio.de

More available books at **www.hansebooks.com**

BANKS AND BANKING

CONTAINING

A FULL ANNOTATION OF

" The Bank Act "

53 VIC. (D.) CHAPTER 31, (1890).

TOGETHER WITH

THOSE SECTIONS OF THE CRIMINAL CODE, 1892, WHICH ARE OF SPECIAL IMPORTANCE TO BANKERS.

SECOND EDITION.

BY

J. J. GORMULLY, Esq.,
One of Her Majesty's Counsel.

AND

R. V. SINCLAIR, Esq.,
Of Osgoode Hall, Barrister-at-law.

OTTAWA :
PRINTED BY A. S. WOODBURN.
1892.

TABLE OF CASES

A.

B.

C.

M.

N.

P.

Q.

R.

BOOKS REFERRED TO.

Abbot's Dig. Corporations.
Angell & Ames on Corporations.
Brice on Ultra Vires.
Civil Code of Lower Canada.
Grant on Banking.
Morse on Banking.
Pothier.
Robinson & Joseph's Digests.
Sheldon on Mortmain.

———————

AN ACT RESPECTING BANKS AND BANKING.

[Assented to 16th May, 1890.]

H ER Majesty, by and with the advice and consent of the Senate and House of Commons of Canada, enacts as follows :—

SHORT TITLE.

1. This Act may be cited as "The Bank Act." (R.S.C. cap. 120, sec. 1.) Short title.

The power to incorporate Banks and to legislate generally in respect of them is expressly conferred on the Parliament of Canada by section 91 of the B. N. A. Act. There have been several cases in which the extent of this power has been considered. See Quirt v. Queen, 19 S. C. R. 510, (1891). Merchants v. Smith, 8, S. C. R. 512, (1884).

As to the power of the Provincial Legislatures to impose taxes on Banks. See Bank of Toronto v. Lambe, 12 App-Cas. 575, (1887).

INTERPRETATION

2. In this Act, unless the context otherwise requires,— Interpretation.

(*a*) The expression "the bank" means any bank to which this Act applies; (R.S.C. cap. 120, sec. 2, ss. e.) "The bank."

"Treasury board."

(*b*) The expression "Treasury Board" means the board provided for by section nine of chapter twenty-eight of the Revised Statutes of Canada, or any Act in amendment thereof or substitution therefor. (New.)

"Goods, wares and merchandise"

(*c.*) The expression "goods, wares and merchandise" includes, in addition to the things usually understood thereby, timber, deals, boards, staves, saw-logs and other lumber, petroleum, crude oil, and all agricultural produce, and other articles of commerce. (R.S. C. cap. 120, sec. 2, ss. a.)

For further notes on this subsection see Sec. 73.

"Warehouse receipt."

(*d.*) The expression "warehouse receipt" means any receipt given by any person for any goods, wares, or merchandise, in his actual, visible and continued possession, as bailee thereof, in good faith, and not as of his own property, and includes receipts given by any person who is the owner or keeper of a harbor, cove, pond, wharf, yard, warehouse, shed, storehouse or other place for the storage of goods, wares or merchandise, for goods, wares and merchandise delivered to him as bailee and actually in the place, or in one or more of the places *owned or* kept by him, whether such person is engaged in other business or not.

The corresponding subsection in the Repealed Act is R. S. C. Cap. 120, Sec. 2, ss. b. The present subsection omits words from and adds words to the repealed subsection.

For notes on the meaning of the expression "warehouse receipt" see Sec. 73.

(e.) The expression "bill of lading" includes all receipts for goods, wares or merchandise, accompanied by an undertaking to transport the same from the place where they were received to some other place, whether by land or water, or partly by land and partly by water, and by any mode of carriage whatever. (R.S.C. cap. 120, sec. 2, ss. c. slightly changed). "Bill of lading."

For further notes on this subsection see sec. 73.

(f.) The word "manufacturer" includes maltsters, distillers, brewers refiners and producers of petroleum, tanners, curriers, packers, canners of meat, pork, fish, fruit or vegetables, and any person who produces by hand, art, process or mechanical means any goods, wares or merchandise. (New.) "Manufacturer."

For notes on this subsection see sec. 74.

APPLICATION OF ACT.

3. The provisions of this Act apply to the several banks enumerated in Schedule A to this Act, and to every bank incorporated after the first day of January, in the year one thousand eight hundred and ninety, whether this Act is specially mentioned in its Act of incorporation or not, but not to any other bank, except as hereinafter specially provided. To what banks the Act applies.

The corresponding section of the old Act is R. S. C. Cap. 120, Sec. 3. The language of the present section is slightly changed to meet the new circumstances.

Charters continued to 1st July, 1901.

4. The charters or Acts of incorporation, and any Acts in amendment thereof, of the several banks enumerated in Schedule A to this Act are continued in force, so far as regards incorporation and corporate name, the amount of capital stock, the amount of each share of such stock and the chief place of business of each bank, until the first day of July, in the year one thousand nine hundred and one, subject to the right of each bank to increase or reduce its capital stock in the manner hereinafter provided ;

As to other particulars.

and as to all other particulars this Act shall form and be the charter of each of the said banks until the said first day of July, in the year one thousand nine hundred and one,— subject in the case of La Banque du Peuple to the provisions hereinafter made in respect to

Proviso: as forfeiture.

that bank : Provided always, that the said charters or Acts of incorporation are hereby continued in force only in so far as they, or any of them, are not forfeited or rendered void under the terms thereof, or of this Act, or of any other Act passed or to be passed, by reason of the non-performance of the conditions thereof, or by insolvency or otherwise.

The corresponding section of the old Act is R. S. C. Cap. 120, Sec. 4. The language of the present section is changed to meet the new circumstances, and a reference is made to the power to reduce the capital stock which is given for the first time by this Act. (See Sec. 28).

5. All the provisions of this Act, except those contained in sections three, six to seventeen (both inclusive), nineteen to twenty-seven (both inclusive), thirty-three, forty-five, and eighty-nine to ninety-six (both inclusive), apply to La Banque du Peuple : Provided that wherever the word " directors " is used in any of the sections which apply to the said bank, it shall be read and construed as meaning the principal partners or members of the corporation of the said bank ; and so much of the Act incorporating the said bank, or of any Act amending or continuing it, as is inconsistent with any section of this Act applying to the said bank, or which makes any provision in any matter provided for by such sections other than is hereby made, is hereby repealed ; otherwise the said Acts are continued in force, subject to the proviso contained in section four of this Act.

What provisions shall apply to La Banque du Peuple.

Proviso: as directors.

Inconsistent enactments repealed.

This is a special section applying to the Banque du Peuple. The corresponding section of the old Act is R. S. C. Cap. 120, S c. 88.

6. The provisions contained in sections two, seven, thirty-seven, forty-seven to eighty-eight (both inclusive), and ninety-seven to one hundred and four (both inclusive), apply to the Bank of British North America and the Bank of British Columbia respectively ; and the provisions contained in the other sections of this Act do not apply to the said banks.

What provisions shall apply to the Banks of British North America and of B. C.

This and the following section are applicable specially to the Bank of British North America and the Bank of British

Columbia, both of which possess English Charters. The corresponding sections are R. S. C. Cap. 120, Secs. 87 and 89

Chief seat of business of the said banks.

7. For the purposes of the several sections of this Act made applicable to the Bank of British North America and the Bank of British Columbia, the chief office of the Bank of British North America shall be the office of the Bank of Montreal, in the Province of Quebec, and the chief office of the Bank of British Columbia shall be the office of the Bank at Victoria, in the Province of British Columbia.

How Merchants' Bank of P.E.I. may come under this Act.

8. The provisions of this Act may be extended to the Merchants' Bank of Prince Edward Island by the Treasury Board, upon the application of the directors of the said bank before the expiration of the present charter of the said bank; and upon publication in the *Canada Gazette* of the resolution of the directors applying hereunder, and of the minute of the Treasury Board thereon allowing such application, the provisions of this Act shall, from the time named in such minute, or if there is no time named therein, from the date of the publication thereof in the *Canada Gazette*, apply to the said bank; and its charter and Act of incorporation, and any Acts in amendment thereof, shall thereupon be extended for the same time and to the extent as if the name of the said bank had been included in Schedule A to this Act. (New).

The provisions of this Act were extended to the Merchants Bank of Prince Edward Island on the 1st of February 1892.

INCORPORATION AND ORGANIZATION OF BANKS.

9. The capital stock of every bank hereafter incorporated, the name of the bank, the place where its chief office is to be situate, and the name of the provisional directors shall be declared in the Act of incorporation of every such bank. (R.S.C. cap. 120, sec. 5, slightly changed.) *Matters to be provided for in special Act.*

2. An Act of incorporation of a bank in the form set forth in Schedule B to this Act shall be construed to confer upon the bank thereby incorporated all the powers, privileges and immunities, and to subject it to all the liabilities and provisions set forth in this Act. (New). *Form of Act of incorporation.*

10. The capital stock of any bank hereafter incorporated shall be not less than five hundred thousand dollars, and shall be divided into shares of one hundred dollars each. (New.) *Capital stock and shares.*

11. The number of provisional directors shall not be less than five nor more than ten, and they shall hold office until directors are elected by the subscribers to the stock, as hereinafter provided. (New.) *Provisional directors.*

12. For the purpose of organizing the bank, the provisional directors may cause stock books to be opened, after giving public notice thereof, —upon which stock books shall be recorded the *Opening of stock books.*

subscriptions of such persons as desire to become shareholders in the bank ; and such books shall be opened at the place where the chief office of the bank is to be situate, and elsewhere, in the discretion of the provisional directors, and may be kept open for such time as they deem necessary, (New).

First meeting of subscribers. **13.** So soon as a sum not less than five hundred thousand dollars of the capital stock of the bank has been *bonâ fide* subscribed, and a sum not less than two hundred and fifty thousand dollars thereof has been paid to the Minister of Finance and Receiver General, the **Notice.** provisional directors may, by public notice, published, for at least four weeks, call a meeting of the subscribers to the said stock, to be held in the place named in the Act of incorporation as the chief place of business of the bank, at such time and at such place therein as set forth in the said notice ; at which meeting the subscribers shall determine the day upon which the annual general meeting of the bank is to be held, and **Election of directors.** shall elect such number of directors, duly qualified under this Act, not less than five nor more than ten, as they think necessary, who shall hold office until the annual general meeting in the year next succeeding their election ; and upon the election of directors as aforesaid the functions of the provisional directors shall cease. (New).

This section provides for the first meeting of shareholders and for fixing the day of the annual meeting and for the election of the first board of directors.

14. The bank shall not issue notes nor commence the business of banking until it has obtained from the Treasury Board a certificate permitting it to do so, and no application for such certificate shall be made until directors have been elected by the subscribers to the stock in the manner hereinbefore provided; and every director, provisional director, or other person, issuing or authorizing the issue of the notes of such bank or transacting or authorizing the transaction of any business in connection with such bank, except such as is hereinbefore provided, before the obtaining of the certificate from the Treasury Board, shall be guilty of an offence against the Act. (New).

Conditions previous to commencing business by new banks.

This section prohibits the commencement of business by the bank until it has obtained a certificate of permission to do so from the Treasury Board.

15. No certificate shall be given by the Treasury Board until it has been shown to the satisfaction of the Board, by affidavit or otherwise, that all the requirements of this Act and of the special Act of incorporation of the bank, as to the payment required to be made to the Minister of Finance and Receiver General, the election of directors, deposit for security for note issue, or otherwise, have been complied with, and that the sum so paid was then held by the Minister of Finance and Receiver General; and no certificate as aforesaid shall be given except within one year from the passing of the Act of incorporation of the bank applying for the said certificate. (New).

When certificate may be granted.

This section prescribes the conditions upon which the Certificate of the Treasury Board referred to in Section 14 will issue. It is important to note that this certificate must be obtained within one year from the passing of the Act of incorporation of the bank, and if not so obtained that the Charter of the bank lapses. (See Section 16).

If certificate is not granted.

16. In the event of the bank not obtaining a certificate from the Treasury Board within one year from the time of the passing of its Act of incorporation, all rights, powers and privileges conferred upon such bank by its Act of incorporation shall thereupon cease and determine and be of no force and effect whatever. (New).

Disposal of amount deposited with Minister of Finance.

17. Upon the issue of the certificate in manner hereinbefore provided. the Minister of Finance and Receiver General shall forthwith pay to the bank the amonnt of money so deposited with him as aforesaid, without interest, after deducting therefrom the amount required to be deposited under section fifty-four of this Act; and in case no certificate is issued by the Treasury Board within the time limited for the issue thereof, the amount so deposited shall be returned to the person depositing the same; but in no case shall the Minister of Finance and Receiver General be under any obligation to see to the proper application of the same in any way. (New).

INTERNAL REGULATIONS.

18. The shareholders of the bank (or, in the case of La Banque du Peuple, the principal partners or members of the corporation thereof,) may regulate by by-law, the following matters incident to the management and administration of the affairs of the bank, that is to say : The day upon which the annual general meeting of the shareholders for the election of directors shall be held ; the record to be kept of proxies, and the time, not exceeding thirty days, within which proxies must be produced and recorded prior to a meeting in order to entitle the holder to vote thereon ; the number of the directors, which shall not be less than five and not more than ten, and the quorum thereof, which shall not be less than three ; their qualification, subject to the provisions hereinafter made ; the method of filling vacancies in the board of directors whenever the same occur during each year, and the time and proceedings for the election of directors, in case of failure of any election on the day appointed for it ; the remuneration of the president, vice-president and other directors ; and the amount of discounts or loans which may be made to directors, either jointly or severally, or to any one firm or person, or to any shareholder, or to corporations.

By-laws may be made.

SHAREHOLDERS' POWERS.

This section is a combination of several sections of the old Act with some changes and additions. (See R. S. C. Cap. 120, Sec. 9, ss. 1 & 3, and Secs. 14 & 16). By it the shareholders are empowered to regulate by by-law certain specified matters, viz :

(1)· The day upon which the annual general meeting of shareholders for the election of directors shall be held. (See also Secs. 13 & 19, ss. 4).

(2) The record to be kept of proxies.

(3) The time, not exceeding 30 days prior to a meeting, within which proxies must be produced and recorded. (See also Sec. 25, ss. 4 & 5).

(4) The number of directors, which shall not be less than five nor more than ten.

(5) The quorum, of directors which shall not be less than three.

(6) The qualification of the directors, which must also conform to certain statutory requirements. (See ss. 3, hereof and Sec. 19, ss. 2).

(7) The filling of vacancies in the Board during each year. (See Sec. 19, ss. 7).

(8) The time and proceedings for the election of directors in case of failure of election on the proper day. (See Sec. 20).

(9) The remuneration of the President, Vice-President and other directors.

(10) The amount of discounts or loans to directors and others. (The aggregate of these have to be shewn in the monthly statement to the government see schedule D.)

The next sub-section empowers the shareholders to establish guarantee and pension funds for bank officials.

Sec. 24, ss. 1, empowers a certain proportion of the shareholders to call a special general meeting.

Sec. 24, ss. 2, by implication empowers the shareholders to remove the President, Vice-President or Directors fo misconduct.

Sec. 26 empowers the shareholders to increase the capital stock.

Sec. 28 empowers the shareholders to reduce the capital stock under certain conditions and restrictions.

2. The shareholders may authorize the directors to establish guarantee and pension funds for the officers and employees of the bank and their families, and to contribute thereto out of the funds of the bank. (New). *Guarantee and pension funds*

The power to create guarantee and pension funds is here expressly conferred and contribution thereto authorized out of the funds of the bank. The prior practice of creating a guarantee fund was however recognised and impliedly legalized by the old Act. (See R. S. C. Cap. 120, Sec. 17) and the prior practice of creating a pension fund is recognized and impliedly legalized by this Act by Sec. 22.

3. Until it is otherwise prescribed by by-law under this section, the by-laws of the bank on any matter which may be regulated by by-law under this section shall remain in force, except as to any provision fixing the qualification of directors at an amount less than that prescribed by this Act; and no person shall be elected or continue to be a director unless he holds stock paid up to the amount required by this Act, or such greater amount as is required by any by-law in that behalf. (R.S.C. cap. 120, sec. 4). *Certain by-laws continued.*

By this clause it is provided that no person shall be elected a director unless at the time of his election he possesses the necessary stock qualification and also that no director shall continue as such unless he continues to possess such stock qualification.

4. The foregoing provisions of this section, touching directors, shall not apply to La Banque du Peuple, which shall in these matters be governed by the provisions of its charter. (R. S.C. cap. 120, sec. 9. ss. 2, slightly changed). *Banque du Peuple excepted.*

Board of directors.

19. The stock, property, affairs and concerns of the bank shall be managed by a board of directors who shall be elected annually in manner hereinafter provided, and shall be eligible for re-election. (R.S.C. cap. 120, sec. 9, ss. 2 and sec. 12).

This clause places the property and business of the bank under the management of the board of directors subject to the control of the shareholders in certain specified matters.

For the powers of the shareholders, see notes to sec. 18.

As to the powers of the directors to make by laws, calls, convene meetings, allot stock, and sue &c., see Section 19, ss. 7, and Sections 22, 23, 24, 27, 29, 30, 31, 32, 33, 39, 46, 47, 58 and 92.

As to the qualifications required by, and the duties and liabilities expressly imposed on directors, see sec. 18, ss. 2, Sec. 19, ss. 2, 4, 6 and 7, and Sections 45, 48, 52, 92, 97 and 99.

As to the quorum of directors, see Section. 18.

A bond may be given up to be cancelled by the president and directors of a banking corporation without their assent being signified under the corporate seal. The Bank of Upper Canada vs. Widmer 2 O. S. 222 (1829).

A director of a company from the time he becomes aware of breaches of trust by his co-directors, incurs liability even though he did not directly sanction them, and may be held personally answerable for any losses sustained thereby, if he remains passive and omits to take proper steps to prevent such misconduct, and to institute if necessary proceedings against his colleagues in default. Jackson vs. The Munster Bank 15 L. R. Ir. 356 (1885).

Qualification.

2. Each director shall hold capital stock of the bank as follows :—When the paid-up capital stock is one million dollars or less, each director shall hold stock on which not less than three thousand dollars has been paid up; when the paid-up capital stock is over one million dollars, and does not exceed three million dollars, each director shall hold stock on which not less than four thousand dollars has been paid up; and when the paid-up capital stock exceeds three million dollars, each director shall hold stock on which not less than five thousand dollars has been paid up: (R.S.C. cap. 120, sec. 9, ss. 2, changed).

By the above sub-section the minimum share qualification of a director is fixed. (See also Section 18).

3. A majority of the directors shall be natural-born or naturalized subjects of Her Majesty: (R.S.C. cap. 120, sec. 12). *Majority to be British subjects.*

4. The directors shall be elected by the shareholders on such day in each year as is appointed by the charter or by any by-law of the bank, and such election shall take place at the head office of the bank at such time of the day as the directors appoint; and public notice thereof shall be given by the directors, by publishing the same for at least four weeks previous to the time of holding such election, in a newspaper published at the place where the said head office is situate: (R.S.C. cap. 120, sec. 12, part, slightly changed). *Election. Notice.*

5. The persons, to the number authorized to be elected, who have the greatest number of votes at any election, shall be directors: (R.S. C. cap. 120, sec. 12, ss. 3, slightly changed). *Who shall be directors.*

Provision in case of equality of votes.

6. If it happens at any election that two or more persons have an equal number of votes and the election or non-election of one or more such persons as a director or directors depends on such equality, then the directors who have a greater number, or the majority of them, shall determine which of the said persons so having an equal number of votes shall be the director or directors, so as to complete the full

Election of dresident, &c.

number; and the said directors, as soon as may be, after the said election, shall proceed to elect, by ballot, two of their number to be president and vice-president respectively : (R.S.C. cap. 120, sec. 12, ss. 4, slightly changed).

Vacancies, how filled.

7 If a vacancy occurs in the board of directors, such vacancy shall be filled in the manner provided by the by-laws; but the non-filling of the vacancy shall not vitiate the acts of a quorum of the remaining directors; and if the vacancy so created is in the office of the president or vice-president, the directors shall, from among themselves, elect a president or vice-president, who shall continue in office for the remainder of the year. (R.S.C. cap. 120, sec. 12, ss. 5, slightly changed).

Section 18 provides that the directors shall not be less than five nor more than ten, and that the quorum shall not be less than three. Where there is a maximum and minimum number of directors fixed by law, then directors cannot act if the number falls below the minimum, Alma Spinning Co. L. R. 16 Chy. Div. 681 (1880), unless as in this sub-section, there is power given to act notwithstanding

vacancies, Scottish Petroleum Co. L R. 23 Chy. Div. 431
(1883). Here the power to act continued as long as there
is a quorum present at a meeting of the board.

20. If an election of directors is not made on Provision in case of failure the day appointed for that purpose, such elec- of election. tion of directors may take place on any other day according to the by-laws made by the shareholders in that behalf; and the directors then in office shall remain in office until a new election is made. (R.S.C. cap. 120, sec. 15, changed).

21. At all meetings of the directors, the Meetings of directors. president, or in his absence the vice-president. or in the absence of both of them, one of the directors present, chosen to act *pro tempore*, Casting vote shall preside; and the president, vice-president of presiding director. or president *pro tempore* so presiding shall vote as a director, and if there is an equal division on any question shall also have a casting vote. (R.S.C. cap. 120, sec. 16, part).

It may be noted that this section gives to the presiding officer of a directors' meeting in addition to his own vote a casting vote in case of an equality of votes.

22. The directors may make by-laws and General regulations (not repugnant to the provisions of directors. this Act or the laws of Canada) touching the management and disposition of the stock, property, affairs and concerns of the bank, and touching the duties and conduct of the officers, clerks and servants employed therein, and all

such other matters as appertain to the business
Proviso ; as to
by-laws in
force. of a bank :   Provided always, that all by-laws
of the bank heretofore lawfully made and now
in force, in regard to any matter respecting which
the directors may make by-laws under this
section (including any by-laws for establishing
guarantee and pension funds for the employees
of the bank), shall remain in force until they
are repealed or altered by others made under
this Act.   (R.S.C. cap. 120, sec. 17, changed).

The power to authorize the creation of pension and guarantee funds is now expressly conferred on the shareholders
by Sec. 18, ss. 2 of this Act.

As to the shareholders' powers to make by-laws see notes
to Sec. 18.

As to the shareholders' power of repealing or changing
existing by-laws that under this Act can only be made by
shareholders, see Sec. 18, ss. 3.

Appointment
of officers, &c. **23**. The directors may appoint as many
officers, clerks and servants for carrying on the
business of the bank, and with such salaries and
allowances, as they consider necessary, and
they may also appoint a director or directors
for any branch of the bank : (R.S.C. cap. 120,
sec. 18).

Security to be
given. 2. Before permitting any cashier, officer,
clerk or servant of the bank to enter upon the
duties of his office, the directors shall require
him to give bond, guarantee, or other security
to the satisfaction of the directors, for the due
and faithful performance of his duties : R.S.C.
cap. 120, sec. 18, ss. 2 slightly changed).

A surety by bond for the due performance of the office of a bank agent is not responsible for losses occurring after the nature of the agency has been changed and the agent appointed a cashier. Bank of Upper Canada v. Covert, 5 O.S. 541 (1834).

In an action on a bond. Plea, that the mode of paying the clerk's salary had been changed from the manner stipulated in the bond. Held, no defence. Bank of Toronto v. Wilmot, 19 U. C. Q. B. 73 (1859).

Where the bond was for due performance of duties as clerk, *or in any other capacity whatsoever*, and it was pleaded that the clerk was, without the defendant's consent, made teller, which was another and more responsible office, and that the defendant was thereby discharged, it was held that this defence was bad. Royal Canadian Bank v. Yates, 19 U. C. C. P. 439 (1869).

In an action against the sureties on a bond guaranteeing the honesty of one M. as cashier, a defence was pleaded by the sureties of neglect of the directors of the bank in not inspecting the books so as to detect any malversation on the part of M. Held, that to sustain this defence the sureties must show connivance or such gross negligence as to warrant the inference of fraud or connivance between the bank and M. A further defence was raised that the cashier had been employed by the directors in unlawful speculations in the stock of the bank and other stocks in the course of which he appropriated to his own use certain funds of the bank kept at special accounts in connection with such speculations.

Held, no defence—as the claim of the bank against the sureties was for moneys so misappropriated and not for losses occasioned by such unlawful speculations.

Exchange Bank vs. Barnes, { 7 O.R., 309 (1884) affirmed.
Exchange Bank vs. Springer, { 13 A.R., 390 (1886)—14
S. C. R 716—(1887).

24. The directors of the bank, or any four of them,—or any number not less than twenty-five of the shareholders of the bank, who are Special general meetings.

together proprietors of at least one-tenth of the paid-up capital stock of the bank, by themselves or by their proxies,—may, at any time, call a special general meeting of the shareholders, to be held at their usual place of meeting, upon giving six weeks' previous public notice, specifying in such notice the object of such meeting: (R.S.C. cap. 120, sec. 11).

It is a general principle of corporation law that the notice convening a meeting should specify in a general way the business intended to be transacted thereat.

Removal of president, director, &c.

2. If the object of any such special general meeting is to consider the proposed removal of the president or vice-president, or of a director of the bank, for maladministration or other specified and apparently just cause, and if a majority of the votes of the shareholders at such meeting is given for such removal, a director to replace him shall be elected or appointed in the manner provided by the by-laws of the bank, or if there are no by-laws providing therefor, then by the shareholders at such meeting; and if it is the president or vice-president who is removed, his office shall be filled by the directors in the manner provided in case of a vacancy occurring in the office of president or vice-president. (R.S.C. cap. 120. sec. 11, ss. 2).

New election.

As to shareholders' powers generally see notes to Sec. 18.

This sub-section gives the shareholders power to remove directors for cause. Without this statutory power it would appear that a company whose directors are appointed for a definite period has no inherent power to remove them before

the expiration of that period. Imperial Hy. Hotel Co.
Blackpool vs. Hampson, L. R. 23 Ch. Div. 1 (1882). See
also Harben vs. Phillips, L. R. 23 Ch. Div. 14 (1883).

25. Every shareholder shall, on all occasions *Votes on shares*
on which the votes of the shareholders are
taken, have one vote for each share held by
him for at least thirty days before the time of
meeting (see also ss. 6 hereof) ; and in all cases *Ballot.*
when the votes of the shareholders are taken,
the voting shall be by ballot : (R.S.C. cap. 120,
sec. 10, ss. 1 part, ss. 4).

2 All questions proposed for the considera- *Majority to*
determine.
tion of the shareholders shall be determined by
the majority of the votes of the shareholders
present in person or represented by proxy ; and
the chairman elected to preside at any such meeting of the shareholders shall vote as a shareholder only, unless there is a tie, —in which case,
except as to the election of a director, he shall *Casting vote.*
have a casting vote : (R.S.C. cap. 120, sec. 10, ss.
2, slightly changed.)

It is important to observe that this clause in case of an
equality of votes gives the chairman of a shareholders
meeting a casting vote on all questions except that of the
election of a director, which is otherwise provided for, see sec.
19 ss. 6.

3. If two or more persons are joint holders *As to joint*
holders of
of shares, any one such joint holder may he *shares.*
empowered, by letter of attorney from the
other joint holder or holders, or a majority of
them, to represent the said shares, and vote
accordingly : (R.S.C. cap. 120, sec. 10 ss. 3).

Proxies.

4. Shareholders may vote by proxy, but no person other than a shareholder eligible to vote, shall be permitted to vote or act as such proxy, and no manager, cashier, clerk or other subordinate officer of the bank shall vote either in person or by proxy, or hold a proxy for that purpose : (R.S.C. cap. 120, sec. 10, ss. 1 part, slightly changed).

It must be noted that by this sub-section the proxy must not only be a shareholder, but a shareholder *eligible to vote* (see ss. 1, 3 & 6 hereof).

As to the proxies see next sub-section and section 18. hereof.

The president of a bank is not prohibited from voting on proxies handed to him by other shareholders. Regina vs. The Bank of Upper Canada, 5 U. C. Q. B., 338 (1849).

Renewal of proxies.

5. No appointment of a proxy to vote at any meeting of the shareholders of the bank shall be valid for that purpose unless it has been made or renewed in writing within the two years next preceding the time of such meeting: (R.S.C. cap. 120, sec. 4, changed).

Under this Act proxies must be renewed every two years instead of three years as prescribed by the repealed Act.

As to the recording of proxies see Sec. 18.

In certain cases calls must be paid before voting.

6. No shareholder shall vote, either in person or by proxy, on any question proposed for the consideration of the shareholders of the bank at any meeting of such shareholders, or in any case in which the votes of the shareholders of the bank are taken, unless he has paid all calls made by the directors which are then due and

payable : (R.S.C. cap. 120, sec. 13, slightly changed).

As to what shareholders are entitled to vote see Sec. 25, ss. 1 and 3.

CAPITAL STOCK.

26. The capital stock of the bank may be increased from time to time, by such percentage or by such amount, as is determined upon by by-law passed by the shareholders, at the annual general meeting, or at any special general meeting called for the purpose : Provided always, that no such by-law shall come into operation, or be of any force or effect, unless and until a certificate approving thereof has been issued by the Treasury Board : (R.S.C. cap. 120. sec. 7 part, changed). *Increase of capital.* *Approval of Treasury Board.*

The proviso at the end of the above section requiring the approval of the Treasury Board is new. For the meaning of the expression " Treasury Board " see sec. 2 ss (b).

As to the powers of shareholders generally, see notes to section 18.

2. No such certificate shall be issued by the Treasury Board unless application therefor is made within three months from the time of the passing of such by-law, nor unless it appears to the satisfaction of the Treasury Board that a copy of such by-law, together with notice of intention to apply for such certificate, has been published for at least four weeks in the *Canada* *Conditions of application for approval.*

Gazette, and in one or more newspapers published in the place where the chief office or place of business of the bank is situate; nothing herein contained, however, shall be construed to prevent the Treasury Board from refusing to issue such certificate if it thinks best so to do. (New).

How stock shall be allotted.

27. Any of the original unsubscribed capital stock, or of the increased stock of the bank, shall, when the directors so determine, be allotted to the then shareholders of the bank *pro ratâ,* and at such rate as is fixed by the directors, but no fraction of a share shall be so allotted; provided that in no case shall a rate be fixed by the directors, which will make the premium (if any) paid or payable on such stock so allotted exceed the percentage which the reserve fund of the bank then bears to the paid-up capital stock thereof; and any of such alloted stock which is not taken up by the shareholder to whom such allotment has been made, within six months from the time when notice of the allotment was mailed to his address, or which he declines to accept, may be offered for subscription to the public, in such manner and on such terms as the directors prescribe. (R.S.C. cap. 120, sec. 8, added to and changed).

The proviso which limits the Directors in fixing the premium price of the stocks to be allotted hereunder is new.

Capital stock may be reduced.

28. The capital stock of the bank may be reduced by by-law passed by the shareholders

at the annual general meeting, or at a special
general meeting called for the purpose ; but no
such by-law shall come into operation or be of
force or effect until a certificate approving
thereof has been issued by the Treasury Board :
(New).

Until the passing of this Act the capital stock of a bank
could only be reduced by Act of Parliament. By this section, however, power to reduce the capital stock is given to
the shareholders to be exercised as provided herein. (See
sections 4 and 48).

2. No such certificate shall be issued by the Treasury
Board unless application therefor is made
within three months from the time of
the passing of the by-law, nor unless it appears
to the satisfaction of the Board that the shareholders voting for such by-law represent a
majority in value of all the shares then issued
by the bank, and that a copy of the by-law,
together with notice of intention to apply to
the Treasury Board for the issue of a certificate
approving thereof, has been published for at
least four weeks in the *Canada Gazette*, and in
one or more newspapers published in the place
where the chief office or place of business of the
bank is situate ; nothing herein contained, however, shall be construed to prevent the Treasury
Board from refusing to issue such certificate if
it thinks best so to do: (New).

Certificate of Treasury Board.

3. In addition to evidence of the passing of
the by-law and the publication thereof in the
manner above provided, statements showing

Statements to be submitted.

the amount of stock issued and the number of shareholders, with the amount of stock held by each, represented at such meeting, and the number of shareholders, with the amount of stock held by each, who voted for such by-law, and also full statements of the assets and liabilities of the bank, together with a statement of the reasons and causes why such reduction is sought, shall be laid before the Treasury Board at the time of the application for the issue of a certificate approving such by-law : (New).

Reduction not to affect liability of share holders. 4. The passing of such by-law, and any reduction of the capital stock of the bank thereunder, shall not, in any way, diminish or interfere with the liability of the shareholders of the bank to the creditors thereof at the time of the issue of the certificate approving such by-law : (New).

If legislation is asked to sanction reduction. 5. If, in any case, legislation is sought to sanction any reduction of the capital stock of any bank, a copy of the by-law or resolution passed by the shareholders in regard thereto, together with statements similar to those above provided to be laid before the Treasury Board, shall be filed with the Minister of Finance and Receiver-General, at least one month prior to the introduction into Parliament of the Bill relating to such reduction : (New).

Limit to reduction. 6. The capital shall not be reduced below the amount of two hundred and fifty thousand dollars of paid-up stock. (New).

SHARES AND CALLS.

29. The shares of the capital stock of the *Shares and transfer there- of.* bank shall be personal estate, and shall be assignable and transferable at the chief place of business of the bank, or at such of its branches, or at such other place or places in the United Kingdom, or in any of the British colonies or possessions, and according to such form, and subject to such rules and regulations, as the directors prescribe; and books of sub- *Books of subscription.* scription may be opened, and the dividends accruing on any shares of such stock may be made payable at any of the places aforesaid; and the directors may appoint such agents in the United Kingdom, or in any of the British colonies or possessions, for the purposes of this section, as they deem necessary. (R. S. C. cap. 120, secs. 19 in part and 29 in part, with additions; see also secs. 35 to 41 of this Act).

SHARES ARE BY THIS CLAUSE DECLARED TRANSFERABLE.

In Smith v. The Bank of Nova Scotia, 8 S.C.R. 558 (1883) it was held, that shares are, by the express provisions of the Bank Act (then 34 V., c. 5, s. 19) transferable at the will of . the holder, and that the directors are bound to register the transfer unless there are debts or liabilities owing by the shareholder to the bank, and that to justify the directors in refusing to register transfers of shares they must bring themselves strictly within the terms of the section, and that a resolution passed at a meeting of directors and shareholders, purporting to restrain for a certain time the transfer of shares, was *ultra vires*, and consequently not binding on dissenting or absent shareholders. See also Barss v. Bank of Nova Scotia, 6 C.L.T. 443 (1885).

Opinions have been recently expressed in the House of Lords in England, that where the stock certificate issued by a bank contains a note that the certificate must be surrendered with the instrument of or at the time of transfer, it would be wrong for the bank to register a transfer until the certificate was produced, or its non-production satisfactorily accounted for. This was decided in the case of a company to which the Companies Clauses Consolidation (Scotland) Acts applied (8 & 9 Vic. ch. 17) the language of section 21 of which is almost identical with section 43 of this Act, it was argued that the directors had no right to hamper the transfer of shares by such a condition or regulation, but Lord Blackburn said he thought they had. See Colonial Bank v. Whinney, L.R. 11 App. Cas. 426 (1886).

WHERE SHARES CAN BE SOLD IN EXECUTION.

In re The Bank of Ontario, 44 U.C.Q.B., 247 (1879).

It did not appear in this case that the Ontario Bank had a share register in Montreal, but it was decided that a sale in execution in the Province of Quebec might be made of shares of this bank whose head office was in Ontario, it appearing that by the law of the Province of Quebec service of process could be legally effected at the branch of such bank in Montreal, and that the Consolidated Statute of Canada, c. 70, is in force in that province, by which statute (section 2) it is provided that where service of process can be legally made on the company, there the shares may be seized and notice given.

Payment of shares.

30. The shares of the capital stock shall be paid in by such instalments and at such times and places as the directors appoint: Provided

always, that the directors may cancel any sub- Proviso : ten
per cent. pay-
able on sub-
scription.
scription for any share unless a sum equal to
ten per cent. at least on the amount subscribed
for is actually paid at the time of, or within
thirty days after, the time of subscribing ; but
such cancellation shall not relieve the subscriber
from his liability to creditors in the event of
insolvency as hereinafter provided. (R. S. C.
cap. 120, sec. 20 changed).

The language of the proviso to sec. 20 of the previous
Bank Act was as follows : " Provided always that no share
shall be held to be lawfully subscribed for unless a sum
equal to at least ten per centum on the amount subscribed
for is actually paid at the time of or within thirty days after
the time of subscribing." Its meaning was discussed in the
winding up proceedings of the Central Bank. Some of the
contributories contended, though unsuccessfully, that if the
ten per cent. on the amount subscribed was not paid at the
time of the original subscription for bank shares or within thirty
days thereafter as required by the above proviso—although
afterwards paid to and accepted by the bank before the first
transfer of the shares took place, subsequent transferees of
the shares could not be placed on the list of contributories
in the winding up. In Baines & Nasmith's case (16 Ont. R.
293, 1888, affd. 16 App. R. 237, 1889, 18 A.R. 209, 1889), the
Chancellor held that the provision as to payment of the ten
per cent. is for the protection of the public, and till payment
is made the person subscribing may not be able to deal with
the stock, but he is at least equitable owner, and may
become legally entitled on making the prescribed payment.
The contention thus put forward by the contributories in
Baines case would not be possible as the law now stands. The
language of the old proviso " no share shall be held to be lawfully subscribed, &c." has been changed, and instead thereof a
power is given to the directors to cancel the subscription, the
subscriber still, however, remaining liable to creditors in the
event of the insolvency of the bank. (See sec. 89 et seq.)

Calls on shares.

31. The directors may make such calls of money from the several shareholders for the time being, upon the shares subscribed for by them respectively, as they find necessary : (R. S.C. cap. 120, sec. 21).

A call was made by four directors, one of whom was not legally appointed. It was held that though one of the directors who joined in making the call was not legally appointed, the call was valid, three of the directors who made it being duly qualified, and that number being sufficient under section 16. Bank of Liverpool v. Bigelow, 3 R. & C. 236, Nova Scotia (1878). The facts on which this decision is founded do not appear very clearly in the report. In Brice on Ultra Vires, 2nd edition, page 362, it is laid down that where the power to make calls is vested in the directors, a call made by those who are actually directors and not yet removed, even though illegally elected, will be good. It would appear, however, from the decision of the Privy Council in The Garden Gully United Quartz Mining Company v. McLister, L.R., 1 App. Cases, 39 (1875), that to justify a forfeiture for non-payment of calls, the calls must have been regularly made by a board of directors who had been duly elected, and this case seems to throw doubt on the validity of calls made by a *de facto* board of directors. See also Bottomley's Case, 16 Ch. Div. 681 (1880). As to the powers and duties of directors to make calls when the bank is insolvent, see section 92.

Time of calls and notice.

2. Such calls shall be made at intervals of not less than thirty days, and upon notice to be given at least thirty days prior to the day on

Limitation.

which such calls shall be payable ; and no such call shall exceed ten per cent. of each share subscribed. (R.S.C. cap. 120, sec. 21, ss. 2).

There must be an interval of not less than thirty days between the making of two successive calls as well as an interval of at least thirty days between the time of making a call and the time fixed for payment thereof.   Robertson v. La Banque d'Hochelaga, 4 L.N. 314 (1881).

32. The directors may, in case of the non- payment of any call, in the corporate name of the bank, sue for, recover. collect and get in all such calls, or may cause and declare such shares to be forfeited to the bank.   (R.S.C. cap. 120, sec. 22, slightly changed). *Recovery of calls.*

See also sections 33 and 34.

This section gives power to the directors to forfeit shares for non-payment of calls.

See Robertson v. Banque d'Hochelaga, 4 L.N. 314 (1881). The plaintiff in this action sought to have restored to him certain shares in the defendant bank, which had been forfeited by the directors for non-payment of calls. The directors on three several occasions notified the plaintiff that unless the calls were paid they would sue him for the amount. Without any further or other notification than this they passed a resolution confiscating the shares. The court decided that the directors having elected to sue could not alter their election and proceed to confiscate the shares without first giving the plaintiff a notice of their intention so to do.

It has been decided that where the holder of stock dies intestate and a call is made thereon after his death, administration will be granted to the nominee of the company as a creditor of the estate of the deceased.   Tomlinson v. Gilby, 54 L.J., 80 (1885).

33 If any shareholder refuses or neglects to pay any instalment upon his shares of the capital stock at the time appointed therefor, such shareholder shall incur a penalty to the use of the bank of a sum of money equal to ten *Forfeiture of shares for non-payment of calls.*

per cent. of the amount of such shares; and if
the directors declare any shares to be forfeited
to the bank they shall within six months thereafter, without any previous formality other than
thirty days' public notice of their intention so
to do, sell at public auction the said shares, or
so many of the said shares as shall, after deducting the reasonable expenses of the sale, yield a
sum of money sufficient to pay the unpaid
instalments due on the remainder of the said
shares and the amount of penalties incurred
upon the whole; and the president or vice-
president, manager or cashier of the bank shall
execute the transfer to the purchaser of the
shares so sold; and such transfer shall be as
valid and effectual in law as if it had been
executed by the original holder of the shares
thereby transferred; but the directors, or the
shareholders at a general meeting, may, notwithstanding anything in this section contained,
remit, either in whole or in part, and condi-
tionally or unconditionally, any forfeiture or
penalty incurred by the non-payment of
instalments as aforesaid, or the bank may
enforce the payment of any call or calls by suit,
instead of declaring the shares forfeited. (R.S.
C. cap. 120, sec. 23, slightly changed).

Under section 32 the directors are empowered to
forfeit shares absolutely in case of non-payment of calls. '
Under this section the shareholder by neglect to pay
calls incurs a forfeiture to the use of the bank of a sum of
money equal to ten per cent. on the amount of his shares;
and the directors are empowered to sell—at public auction

on giving thirty days' prior public notice of sale—the said shares or so many of them as shall, after deducting reasonable expenses of sale, yield sufficient to pay the unpaid instalments due on the remainder thereof and the amount of forfeitures incurred on the whole.

Section 33 would, therefore, seem to limit to the extent therein provided the apparently larger right of forfeiture given by section 32.

As to forfeiture for non-payment when bank is insolvent. (See secs. 92 to 94).

Under this and also the preceding section the directors are empowered to sue the shareholders for the amount due on any call.

It would seem, however, that the directors have no power to forfeit and to sue. The power is apparently conferred in the alternative—either to forfeit or sue. See Robertson v. La Banque d'Hochelaga (1881), cited in note to section 32.

34. In any action brought to recover any money due on any such call it shall not be necessary to set forth the special matter in the declaration or statement of claim, but it shall be sufficient to allege that the defendant is holder of one share or more, as the case may be, in the capital stock of the bank, and is indebted to the bank for a call or calls upon such share or shares, in the sum to which the call or calls amount, as the case may be, stating the amount and number of such calls, whereby an action has accrued to the bank to recover the same from such defendant by virtue of this Act; and it shall not be necessary to prove the appointment of the directors. (R.S.C. cap. 120, sec. 22, ss. 2, changed).

Recovery by suit.

What only need be proved.

TRANSFER AND TRANSMISSION OF SHARES.

35. No assignment or transfer of the shares of the capital stock of the bank shall be valid unless it is made and registered and accepted by the person to whom the transfer is made, in a book or books kept for that purpose, nor unless the person making the same has, if required by the bank, previously discharged all his debts or liabilities to the bank which exceed in amount the remaining stock. if any, belonging to such person, valued at the then current rate ; and no fractional part of a share, or less than a whole share, shall be assignable or transferable. (R.S.C. cap. 120, sec. 29, in part).

Conditions of transfer of shares.

Fraction of share not transferable

In the liquidation of the Central Bank (a bank having its head office in the Province of Ontario) the evidence showed that the bank had adopted the practice of dealing with its shares by way of marginal transfer, that the first transferor executed a transfer in blank, subject as by marginal note, initialed by him, to the order of a broker, and that the ultimate purchaser signed an acceptance in the transfer book immediately under the transfer so signed in blank by the first transferor, the intermediate dealing of the broker being omitted from extended record in the bank books, and the ultimate purchaser being duly entered as a shareholder in the stock ledger of the bank :—Held, that this amounted substantially to an acceptance of shares transferred in blank, which was lawful where transfer by deed was not prescribed, and the entry in the stock ledger amounted to registration within the meaning of the Act.

Where it appeared that in one such case the transferee did not sign the acceptance, but that he subsequently dealt with the shares by selling and transferring them :—

Held, that the transferees from him were properly placed upon the list of contributories, notwithstanding anything in the corresponding section of the Act then in force :—In re-Central Bank-Baines & Nasmiths case 16 Ont. R. 293 (1888) affirmed in App. 16 App. R. 237 (1889); 18 App. R. 209 (1891).

After a winding up order has been made it is too late for holders of shares, entered as such in the books of the bank, to escape liability by showing irregularities in transfers to more or less remote predecessors in title. A loan company which advances money on the security of shares, which are transferred to and accepted by it in the ordinary absolute form cannot escape liability on the ground that it is merely a trustee for the borrower.—In re Central Bank of Canada-Home Savings and Loan Company's case 18 Ont. Appeal Reports 489 (1891).

An infant, however, may repudiate his liability as a contributory,—thus when the infant's father signed her name to a stock subscription book of a bank, paid the calls, and received the dividend cheques, which were endorsed by her at her father's request, the moneys being received by him, and the bank was put into liquidation by winding up proceedings, and the order for call against contributories was made three months before she came of age ; and a year after the liquidation commenced she took proceedings to have her name removed from the list of contributories :—Held, that she was not liable as a contributory and that her name must be removed from the list. In re Central Bank-Hoggs case 19 Ont. R. 7 (1890).

Where an intending purchaser of stock enquired of the bank officers what claims the bank held against such stock, and certain information was given, but before the arrangement for the transfer of the stock was completed another claim, which was then current in one of the other agencies of the bank, was returned unpaid :—Held, that the bank had a right to retain its lien on the stock for the additional sum before allowing the transfer of the stock in its books :—Cook

v. Royal Canadian Bank, 20 Chy., 1 (1873). See also sections 29, 37, 38 and 65.

Transferors of shares whose transfers have been registered within sixty days of the suspension of payment by the bank remain liable for calls. See sections 89 and 96.

By the combined effect of this section and section 65 the bank is entitled to a lien upon the shares of any shareholder for any debt or liability for any debt to the bank and whether matured or only maturing—and may decline to permit any transfer of such shareholder's shares until payment of such debt.

36. A list of all transfers of shares registered each day in the books of the bank, showing the parties to such transfers and the number of shares transferred in each case, shall be made up at the end of each day and kept at the chief place of business of the bank, for the inspection of its shareholders. (R.S.C. cap. 120, sec. 30).

List of transfers to be kept

37. All sales or transfers of shares, and all contracts and agreements in respect thereof, hereafter made or purporting to be made, shall be null and void (saving however, as to a purchaser not having knowledge of the defect, his rights and remedies under the contract of sale), unless the person making such sale or transfer, or in whose name or on whose behalf the same is made, is at the time thereof the registered owner in the books of the bank of the share or shares so sold or transferred, or intended or purported so to be, or has the registered owner's assent to the sale, and the distinguishing number or numbers of such share or shares, if

Transferrer of shares must be registered owner.

any, shall be designated in the contract or agreement of sale or transfer; and any person, whether principal, broker or agent, who violates the provisions of this section by wilfully selling or transferring, or attempting to sell or transfer, any share or shares by a false number, or of which the principal is not, at the time of such sale or attempted sale, the registered owner, or acting with the registered owner's assent to the sale, shall be guilty of an offence against this Act. (New).

This is a new section and is intended to prevent as much as possible the rigging of the market and the trafficking in bank shares.

38. When any share of the capital stock has been sold under a writ of execution, the officer *Sale of shares under execution.* by whom the writ was executed shall, within thirty days after the sale, leave with the bank an attested copy of the writ, with the certificate of such officer endorsed thereon, certifying to whom the sale has been made; and thereupon (but not until after all debts and liabilities of the holder of the share to the bank, and all liens existing in favor of the bank thereon, have been discharged, as herein provided), the president, vice-president, manager or cashier of the bank shall execute the transfer of the share so sold to the purchaser; and such transfer shall be, to all intents and purposes, as valid and effectual in law as if it had been executed by the holder of the said share. (R.S.C. cap. 120, sec. 31, slightly changed).

By 34 Vic., c. 5, s. 19. the   sheriff   was the   officer
empowered to sell shares under a writ of execution.   But it
was, notwithstanding, held in *In re* The Bank of Ontario,
44 U.C.Q.B., 250 (1879), that an execution from the Superior
Court of Montreal might be validly executed by a sworn
bailiff of the court instead of by the sheriff, and the bailiff
might fulfil the duties imposed on the sheriff by that section,
it appearing that under the law of the Province of Quebec
the bailiff is authorized to act and sell in the same way as
the sheriff.   This last point would not arise under this section
as now worded.

Cook v. Royal Canadian Bank, 20 Chy., (1873), and
notes to section 35 and section 65.

39. If the interest in any share in the capital
stock becomes transmitted in consequence of
the   death,   bankruptcy,   or   insolvency   of
any shareholder, or in consequence of the
marriage of a female shareholder, or by any
other lawful means than by a transfer according
to the provisions of this Act, such transmission
shall be authenticated by a declaration in
writing, as hereinafter mentioned, or in such
other manner as the directors of the bank
require ; and every such declaration shall
distinctly state the manner in which and the
person to whom such shares have been transmitted, and shall be made and signed by such
person ; and the person making and signing
such declaration shall acknowledge the same
before a judge of a court of record, or before
the mayor, provost or chief magistrate of a city,
town, borough or other place, or before a notary
public, where the same is made and signed;
and every declaration so signed and acknowl-

Transmission of shares otherwise than by transfer, how authenti-cated.

edged shall be left with the cashier, manager or
other officer or agent of the bank, who shall
thereupon enter the name of the person entitled
under such transmission in the register of shareholders; and until such transmission has been
so authenticated, no person claiming by virtue
of any such transmission shall be entitled to
participate in the profits of the bank, or to vote
in respect of any such share of the capital
stock: Provided always, that every such *Proviso: as to declaration made out of Canada, &c.*
declaration and instrument as, by this and the
next following section of this Act, are required
to perfect the transmission of a share in the
bank which is made in any country other than
Canada, or any other British colony, or the
United Kingdom, shall be further authenticated
by the clerk of a court of record and under the
seal of such court, or by the British consul or
vice-consul, or other accredited representative
of the British Government in the country
where the declaration is made, or shall be made
directly before such British consul or vice-
consul or other accredited representative ; and
provided also, that the directors, cashier or *Proviso: further evidence may be required.*
other officer or agent of the bank may require
corroborative evidence of any fact alleged in
any such declaration.   (R.S.C. cap. 120, sec. 32,
slightly changed).

40. If the transmission of any share of the
capital stock has taken place by virtue of the *Transmission by marriage of female shareholder*
marriage of a female shareholder, the declara-
tion shall be accompanied by a copy of the

register of such marriage, or other particulars of the celebration thereof, and shall declare the identity of the wife with the holder of such share, and shall be made and signed by such female shareholder and her husband ; and they may include therein a declaration to the effect that the share transmitted is the separate property and under the sole control of the wife, and that she may receive and grant receipts for the dividends and profits accruing in respect thereof, and dispose of and transfer the share itself, without requiring the consent or authority of her husband ; and such declaration shall be binding upon the bank and persons making the same, until the said persons see fit to revoke it by a written notice to that effect to the bank ; but the omission of a statement in any such declaration that the wife making the same is duly authorized by her husband to make the same shall not invalidate the declara·tion. (R.S.C. cap. 120, sec. 33).

Transmission by decease.   **41.** If the transmission has taken place by virtue of any testamentary instrument, or by intestacy, the probate of the will, or the letters of administration, or act of curatorship or tutorship, or an official extract therefrom, shall, together with such declaration, be produced and left with the cashier or other officer or agent of the bank, who shall, thereupon, enter in the register of shareholders the name of the person entitled under such transmission. (R.S.C. cap. 120, sec. 34).

42. If the transmission of any share of the capital stock has taken place by virtue of the decease of any shareholder, the production to the directors and the deposit with them of an authentic notarial copy of the will of the deceased shareholder, if such will is in notarial form according to the law of the Province of Quebec, or of any authenticated copy of the probate of the will of the deceased shareholder, or of letters of administration of his estate, or of letters of verification of heirship, or of the act of curatorship or tutorship, granted by any court in Canada having power to grant the same, or by any court or authority in England, Wales, Ireland, or any British colony, or of any testament testamentary or testament dative expede in Scotland, or, if the deceased shareholder died out of Her Majesty's dominions, the production to and deposit with the directors of any authenticated copy of the probate of his will or letters of administration of his property, or other document of like import, granted by any court or authority having the requisite power in such matters, shall be sufficient justification and authority to the directors for paying any dividend, or for transferring or authorizing the transfer of any share, in pursuance of and in conformity to such probate, letters of administration, or other such document as aforesaid. (R.S.C. cap. 120, sec. 34, changed).

This section gives more specific directions than its predecessors as to the proofs to be produced hereunder.

Bank not bound to see to trusts of its shares.

43. The bank shall not be bound to see to the execution of any trust, whether express, implied or constructive, to which any share of its stock is subject; and the receipt of the person in whose name any such share stands in the books of the bank, or, if it stands in the name of more persons than one, the receipt of one of such persons shall be a sufficient discharge to the bank for any dividend or any other sum of money payable in respect of such share, unless express notice to the contrary has been given to the bank; and the bank shall not be bound to see to the application of the money paid upon such receipt, whether given by one of such persons or all of them. (R.S.C. cap. 120, sec. 37.)

This section deals with trusts to which shares may be subject—see also sections 29, 35 & 36. As to trusts to which deposits may be subject, see section 84, ss. 2.

Under 25 and 26 Vic., cap. 89, sec. 30 (imp.) "The Company's Act, 1862" which is as follows: "No notice of any trust, expressed, implied, or constructive, shall be entered on the register, or be receivable by the registrar, in the case of Companies under this Act," it was decided that where the owner of shares at different times makes in favor of each of two persons, an equitable assignment of such shares, such assignments rank according to their respective dates, and the second transferee by giving notice of his assignment to the bank, before the first transferee does so, does not thereby acquire any priority over the first transferee because to hold otherwise would be to convert the bank into a trustee and to bind it with the notice of a trust. Société Generale de Paris vs. Walker, L.R. 11 App. Cases, 20 (1885) affirming S.C. in L.R. 14 Q.B.D. 426.

From the opinions expressed by the Lord Justices in the above case it would seem that section 43 of this Act on this point would probably receive a similar interpretation to that placed upon section 30 of the Companies Act, 1862. It will of course be observed that section 44 of this Act evidently contemplates the entry of trusts to some extent on the books of the bank.

Now if a share stands on the books of the bank, earmarked with a trust—or, if stands on its books, not so earmarked but the bank has in fact received actual notice that such share is affected by a trust, is it lawful for the bank to allow a transfer of the same, without the concurrence of any one except the person in whose name the share stands in the books of the bank? This is a very important question. It is conceived that the bank will be safe, if the transfer is executed by the person who is the registered shareholder. It has been the universal practice and rightly so, as we think, to act upon transfers so executed. But Mr. Justice Lindley in the case cited in his judgment says: "I have no doubt that if directors allow a transferor to make a transfer which they know to be fraudulent they could be made liable for the value of the shares transferred; they would make themselves parties to his fraud. Moreover, a refusal by directors, or an omission on their part, to pay attention to a notice given to them by a person having an equitable interest in shares, and requiring the directors not to register a transfer for such time as may be necessary to allow him time to apply for a proper restraining order, would be *prima facie* improper. Such conduct on the part of directors, unless explained, would be strong evidence of fraud on their part. But this is quite consistent with holding companies not bound to take notice of equitable interests in shares, not followed up by proceedings to restrain a transfer."

Though a bank is not bound to see to the execution of any trust in regard to its own shares—it, like all other persons, is bound by notices of trust in respect of shares which may be accepted by it as collateral security for advances.

There have been several important cases decided on this point quite recently,—In the bank of Montreal vs. Sweeny, L.R. 12 App. Cases 617 (1887), where shares of a Rolling

Mill Co. stood in the name of one Rose, in trust, and he
transferred the same to the bank as security for a debt which
he owed to it, the Privy Council decided that the bank
had express notice that, as regards the shares transferred to
it, Rose stood to some person in the relation expressed by
the words "in trust," and it was the duty of the bank to decline to take the shares until it had ascertained that Rose's
transfer was authorized by the nature of the trust, and as
Rose had no authority to make such a transfer, the bank
could not retain the shares against the person proved to be
beneficially entitled to them and for whom Rose held them
in trust; see also Raphael vs. McFarlane, 18 S.C.R. 183
(1890); Petry vs. La Caisse D'Economie, 19 S.C.R. 713
(1891). Duggan vs. London & Canadian Loan & Agency
Co. 19 O.R. 272 (1890); 18 A.R. 305 (1891); 20 S.C.R.
481 (1892); Earl of Sheffield vs. London Joint Stock Bank,
13 App. Cas. 333 (1888); London Joint Stock Bank vs.
Simmons, 1892, App. Cas. 201.

44. No person holding stock in the bank as
executor, administrator, guardian or trustee, of
or for any person named in the books of the
bank as being so represented by him, shall be
personally subject to any liability as a shareholder, but the estate and funds in his hands
shall be liable in like manner and to the same
extent as the testator, intestate, ward or person
interested in such trust fund would be, if living
and competent to hold the stock in his own
name; and if the trust is for a living person,
such person shall also himself be liable as a
shareholder; but if such testator, intestate,
ward or person so represented is not so named
in the books of the bank, the executor, administrator, guardian or trustee shall be personally

Executors and trustees not personally liable.

Exception.

liable in respect of such stock as if he held it in
his own name as owner thereof.

In order to exempt the executor, administrator, guardian
or trustee from personal liability under this section, the name
of the testator, intestate, ward or person beneficially interested must appear on the books of the bank. After the City of
Glasgow Bank failure the personal liability of Trustee Shareholders was brought prominently before the public and led,
it is believed, to the adding of this clause to the Bank Act.
See Muir vs. City of Glasgow Bank, L R. 4 App. Cas. ~~437~~ 337/
(1879).

ANNUAL STATEMENT AND INSPECTION.

45. At every annual meeting of the shareholders for the election of directors, the out-
going directors shall submit a clear and full
statement of the affairs of the bank, containing
on the one part,— Statement to be laid before annual meet-ing.

The amount of the capital stock paid in, the
amount of notes of the bank in circulation. the
net profits made, the balances due to other
banks, and the cash deposited in the bank, distinguishing deposits bearing interest from those
not bearing interest; and on the other part,— Liabilities.

The amount of the current coin, the gold and
silver bullion, and the Dominion notes held by
the bank, the balances due to the bank from
other banks, the value of the real and other
property of the bank, and the amount of debts Assets.

owing to the bank, including and particulariz-
ing the amounts so owing upon bills of exchange, discounted notes, mortgages and other
securities,—

Exhibiting, on the one hand, the liabilities
of, or the debts due by the bank, and on the
other hand the assets and resources thereof;
and the said statement shall also exhibit the
rate and amount of the last dividend declared by
the directors, the amount of reserved profits at
the date of such statement, and the amount of
debts due to the bank, over-due and not paid,
with an estimate of the loss which will probably
accrue thereon. (R.S.C. cap. 120, sec. 24,
changed.)

46. The books, correspondence and funds of
the bank shall, at all times, be subject to the
inspection of the directors; but no person, who
is not a director, shall be allowed to inspect the
account of any person dealing with the bank.
(R S.C. cap. 120, sec. 25).

In an action against the sureties on a bond guaranteeing the honesty of one M. as cashier, a defence was pleaded
by the sureties of neglect of the directors of the bank in not
inspecting the books so as to detect any malversation on the
part of M.   Held, that to sustain this defence the sureties
must show connivance or such gross negligence as to warrant
the inference of fraud or connivance between the bank and M.

Exchange Bank vs. Barnes,   } 7 O.R., 309 (1884). aff'd.
Exchange Bank vs. Springer, } 13 A.R., 390 (1886),
                              } 14 S.C.R. 716 (1887).

DIVIDENDS.

47. The directors of the bank shall, subject to the provisions of this Act, declare quarterly or halfyearly dividends of so much of the profits of the bank as to the majority of them seems advisable; and they shall give at least thirty days' public notice of the payment of such dividends previously to the date fixed for such payment; and they may close the transfer books during a certain time, not exceeding fifteen days, before the payment of each dividend. (R.S.C. cap. 120, sec. 9 part, sec. 26 part, slightly changed). Dividends.

The restrictions imposed on directors in connection with the declaration of dividends are contained in the next two sections, viz :—Sections 48 and 49.

48. No dividend cr bonus shall ever be declared so as to impair the paid-up capital; and if any dividend or bonus is so declared or made payable, the directors who knowingly and wilfully concur therein shall be jointly and severally liable for the amount thereof as a debt due by them to the bank; and if any part of the paid-up capital is lost, the directors shall, if all the subscribed stock is not paid up, forthwith make calls upon the shareholders to an amount equivalent to such loss; and such loss and the calls, if any, shall be mentioned in the next re- Dividend not to impair capital. Capital lost to be made up

Proviso turn made by the bank to the Minister of Finance and Receiver-General : Provided that, in any case in which the capital has been impaired as aforesaid, all net profits shall be applied to make good such loss. (R.S.C. cap. 120, sec. 27).

When a bank has impaired its paid-up capital by losses it is expressly forbidden by the proviso at the end of the above section to pay any dividend until such impairment has been made good. Consequently, heretofore the bank has generally made application to Parliament to reduce its capital so as to enable it to go on paying dividends. By this Act, however, power is given to the shareholders to reduce the capital of the bank by by-law. See sections 4 and 28.

Dividend limit-
c: unless there
is a certain re-
serve **49.** No division of profits, either by way of dividends or bonus, or both combined, or in any other way, exceeding the rate of eight per cent per annum, shall be made by the bank, unless, after making the same, it has a rest or reserve fund equal to at least thirty per cent of its paid-up capital ; and all bad and doubtful debts shall be deducted before the amount of such rest is calculated. (R.S.C. cap. 120, sec. 28, slightly changed).

RESERVES.

50. The bank shall hold not less than forty *Part of reserve to be in Dominion notes.* per cent of its cash reserves in Dominion notes; and every bank holding at any time a less amount of its cash reserves in Dominion notes than is prescribed by this section shall incur a penalty of five hundred dollars for each and every violation of the provisions of this section : *Penalty for non-compliance.* (R.S.C. cap. 120, sec. 39 part, slightly changed).

2. The Minister of Finance and Receiver General shall make such arrangements as are *Supply of Dominion notes.* necessary for insuring the delivery of Dominion notes to any bank, in exchange for an equivalent amount of specie, at the several offices at which Dominion notes are redeemable, in the cities of Toronto, Montreal, Halifax, St. John, N.B., Winnipeg, Charlottetown and Victoria, respectively ; and such notes shall be redeemable at the office for redemption of Dominion notes in the place where such specie is given in exchange. (R.S.C. cap. 120, sec. 39, ss. 2 added to).

As to issue and payment of Dominion notes generally, see Revised Statutes of Canada, cap. 31.

NOTE ISSUE.

51. The bank may issue and re-issue notes
Amount and denomination of bank notes. payable to bearer on demand and intended for
circulation; but no such note shall be for a sum
less than five dollars, or for any sum which is
not a multiple of five dollars, and the total
amount of such notes, in circulation at any time,
shall not exceed the amount of the unimpaired
paid-up capital of the bank : (R.S.C. cap. 120,
sec. 40, changed).

Note issue of Banque ou Peuple and Bank of British North America. 2. Notwithstanding anything contained in
the next preceding sub-section, the total
amount of such notes in circulation at any time
of La Banque du Peuple and the Bank of British North America respectively shall not exceed
seventy-five per cent of the unimpaired paid-up
capital of such banks respectively, but each of
such banks may issue such notes in excess of the
said seventy-five per cent upon depositing, with
respect to such excess, with the Minister of
Finance and Receiver General, in cash or bonds
of the Dominion of Canada, an amount equal to
the excess; provided always that in no case
shall the total amount of the notes of either of
the said banks in circulation at any time exceed
the unimpaired paid-up capital of such bank;
and the cash or bonds so deposited shall be
available by the Minister of Finance and
Receiver General for the redemption of notes
issued in excess as aforesaid, in the event of the

suspension of the said banks respectively: (New).

3. If the total amount of the notes of the bank in circulation at any time exceeds the amount authorized by this section, the bank shall incur penalties as follows: If the amount of such excess is not over one thousand dollars, a penalty equal to the amount of such excess; if the amount of such excess is over one thousand dollars and is not over twenty thousand dollars, a penalty of one thousand dollars; if the amount of such excess is over twenty thousand dollars and is not over one hundred thousand dollars, a penalty of ten thousand dollars; if the amount of such excess is over one hundred thousand dollars and not over two hundred thousand dollars, a penalty of fifty thousand dollars; and if the amount of such excess is over two hundred thousand dollars, a penalty of one hundred thousand dollars: (R.S.C. cap. 120, sec. 40, ss. 2, changed.) *Penalties for excess of circulation.*

4. All notes heretofore issued or re-issued by the bank, and now in circulation, which are for a sum less than five dollars, or for a sum which is not a multiple of five dollars, shall be called in and cancelled as soon as practicable. (R.S.C. cap. 120, part of sec. 40.) *Notes under $5 to be called in.*

52. The bank shall not pledge, assign, or hypothecate its notes; and no advance or loan made on the security of the notes of a bank *Pledging of notes prohibited.*

shall be recoverable from the bank or its assets: (New).

This sub-section strikes at and prohibits the creation of preferences by the transfer of blocks of bank notes by the bank officers by way of pledge or assignment or hypothecation.

Penalty for pledging.

2. Every person who, being the president, vice-president, director, principal partner *en commandite*, general manager, manager, cashier, or other officer of the bank, pledges, assigns, or hypothecates, or authorizes, or is concerned in the pledge, assignment or hypothecation of the notes of the bank, and every person who accepts, receives or takes, or authorizes or is concerned in the acceptance or receipt or taking of such notes as a pledge, assignment or hypothecation, shall be liable to a fine of not less than four hundred dollars and not more than two thousand dollars, or to imprisonment for not more than two years, or to both: (New).

Penalty for improper issue or taking of notes.

3. Every person who, being the president, vice-president, director, principal partner *en commandite*, general manager, manager, cashier, or other officer of a bank, with intent to defraud, issues or delivers, or authorizes or is concerned in the issue or delivery of notes of the bank intended for circulation and not then in circulation,—and every person who, with knowledge of such intent, accepts, receives or takes, or authorizes or is concerned in the acceptance, receipt or taking of such notes,—shall be guilty of a mis-demeanor, and liable to im-

prisonment for a term not exceeding seven years, or to a fine not exceeding two thousand dollars, or to both. (New.)

The currency of this country consisting substantially of the notes of chartered banks, this act contains several provisions for increasing the circulating power thereof and in the event of the insolvency of the bank for ensuring the payment of the same. (See secs. 53, 54, 55, 56.) These provisions it is believed will prove sufficient for the purpose, but they were only designed to ensure payment of notes bonâ fide in circulation and performing the functions of currency or money.

53. The payment of the notes issued or re-issued by the bank and intended for circulation, and then in circulation, together with any interest paid or payable thereon as hereinafter provided, shall be the first charge upon the assets of the bank in case of its insolvency; and the payment of any amount due to the Government of Canada, in trust or otherwise, shall be the second charge upon such assets; and the payment of any amount due to the Government of any of the Provinces, in trust or otherwise, shall be the third charge upon such assets: (R.S C. cap. 120, sec. 79, added to.)

Notes to be first charge on assets.

In cases of insolvency of the bank this section makes the "notes in circulation" a first charge upon its assets and then declares that the Dominion Government's indebtedness shall be the second charge and the Provincial Government's indebtedness the third charge. The priority of Crown debts on the bank's assets now depends on this legislation. See cases on this question decided prior hereto—Exchange Bank vs. Queen (Quebec) L.R., 11. App. Cas. 157 (1886)

Queen vs. Bank of Nova Scotia (P.E.I.) 11 S.C.R. 1 (1885), Liquidators Maritime Bank vs. Queen (N.B.) 17 S.C.R. 657 (1889). (This last case deals with moneys held in trust by the Crown as represented by the Dominion Government.) Liquidators Maritime Bank vs. Queen (N.B.) App. Cas., (1892).

2. The amount of any penalties for which the bank is liable shall not form a charge upon the assets of such bank, in case of its insolvency, until all other liabilities are paid. (New.)

Liability for penalties in case of insolvency

54. Every bank to which this Act applies, and which is carrying on its business at the time when this Act comes into force, shall, within fifteen days thereafter, pay to the Minister of Finance and Receiver General, a sum of money equal to two and one-half per cent. of the average amount of its notes in circulation during the twelve months next preceding the date of the coming into force of this Act, or if such bank has not been in operation for twelve months, a sum of money equal to two and one-half per cent. of the average amount of its notes in circulation during the time it has been in operation; and each bank shall, within fifteen days, from and after the first day of July, in the year one thousand eight hundred and ninety-two, pay to the Minister of Finance and Receiver General such further sum of money as is necessary to make the total amount so paid by each bank to be a sum equal to five per cent. of the average amount of its notes in cir-

Existing banks to make deposit with the Minister of Finance equal to five per cent of note circulation.

culation during the twelve months next preceding the date last mentioned,—which sum
shall be adjusted annually as hereinafter provided: (New.)

2. The Merchants' Bank of Prince Edward
Island shall, on or before the day upon which
it becomes subject to the provisions of this Act,
pay to the Minister of Finance and Receiver
General such sum as appears to the satisfaction
of the Treasury Board to be equal to two and
one-half per cent. of the average amount of its
notes in circulation during the then preceding
twelve months; and shall further pay to the
Minister of Finance and Receiver General,
within fifteen days from and after the first day
of July in the year then next following, such
further sum as is necessary to make the total
sum paid by the said bank to be a sum equal
to five per cent. of the average amount of its
notes in circulation from the time the said bank
became subject to the provisions of this Act to
the said first day of July,—which sum shall be
adjusted annually as hereinafter provided:
(New.)

3. The Minister of Finance and Receiver
General shall, upon the issue of a certificate
under this Act authorizing a bank to issue notes
and commence the business of banking, retain
out of any moneys of such bank then in his
possession the sum of five thousand dollars,—
which sum shall be held for the purposes of this

section, until the annual adjustment hereunder takes place in the year then next following, at which time the amount at the credit of the bank shall be adjusted by payment to or by the bank of such sum as is necessary to make the amount at the credit of the bank to be a sum of money equal to five per cent. of the average amount of its notes in circulation from the time it commenced business to the time of such adjustment,—which sum shall be adjusted annually as hereinafter provided : (New.)

Formation of circulation redemption fund.

4. The amounts so paid, retained, and kept on deposit as aforesaid shall form a fund to be known as " The Bank Circulation Redemption Fund,"—which fund shall be held for the following purpose, and for no other, namely : In the event of the suspension by the bank of payment in specie or Dominion notes of any of its liabilities as they accrue, for the payment of the notes then issued or re-issued by such bank, and intended for circulation, and then in circulation, and interest thereon ; and the Minister of Finance and Receiver General shall, with respect to all notes paid out of the said fund, have the same rights as any other holder of the notes of the bank : (New.)

Fund to bear interest.

5. The fund shall bear interest at the rate of three per cent. per annum, and it shall be adjusted, as soon as possible after the thirtieth day of June in each year, in such a way as to make the amount at the credit of each bank

contributing thereto, unless herein otherwise specially provided, equal to five per cent. of the average note circulation of such bank during the then next preceding twelve months: (New.)

6. The average note circulation of a bank during any period shall be determined from the average of the amount of its notes in circulation, as shown by the monthly returns for such period made by the bank to the Minister of Finance and Receiver General; and where, in any return, the greatest amount of notes in circulation at any time during the month is given, such amount shall, for the purposes of this section, be taken to be the amount of the notes of the bank in circulation during the month to which such return relates: (New.)

Note circulation, how determined.

7. In the event of the suspension by the bank of payment in specie or Dominion notes of any of its liabilities as they accrue, the notes of such bank, issued or re-issued and intended for circulation, and then in circulation, shall bear interest at the rate of six per cent. per annum, from the day of such suspension to such day as is named by the directors, or by the liquidator, receiver, assignee or other proper official, for the payment thereof,—of which day notice shall be given by advertisement for at least three days in a newspaper published in the place in which the head office of the bank is situate; but in case any notes presented for payment on or after any day named for pay-

Notes of bank suspending payment to bear interest until redeemed.

ment thereof are not paid, all notes then unpaid and in circulation shall continue to bear
interest to such further day as is named for
payment thereof,—of which day notice shall be
given in manner above provided : Provided

always, that in case of failure on the part of
the directors of the bank, or of the liquidator,
receiver, assignee or other proper official, to
make arrangements within two months from
the day of suspension of payment by the bank
as aforesaid for the payment of all its notes and
interest thereon, the Minister of Finance and
Receiver General may thereupon, make arrangements for the payment of the notes remaining
unpaid, and all interest thereon, out of the
said fund, and shall give such notice of such
payment as he thinks expedient, and on the
day named by him for such payment all interest
on such notes shall cease, anything herein contained to the contrary notwithstanding ; but

nothing herein contained shall be construed to
impose any liability on the Government of Canada or on the Minister of Finance and Receiver
General beyond the amount available from
time to time out of the said fund :   (New.)

8. All payments made from the said fund shall
be without regard to the amount contributed
thereto by the bank in respect of whose notes
the payments are made ; and in case the payments from the fund exceed the amount contributed by such bank to the fund, and all
interest due or accruing due to such bank there-

on, the other banks shall, on demand, make good to the fund the amount of such excess, *pro rota* to the amount which each bank has at that time contributed to the fund ; and all amounts recovered and received by the Minister of Finance and Receiver General from the bank on whose account such payments were made shall, after the amount of such excess has been made good as aforesaid, be distributed among the banks contributing to make good such excess *pro rata* to the amount contributed by each : Provided always, that each of such other banks Proviso. shall only be called upon to make good to the said fund its share of such excess, in payments not exceeding in any one year one per cent of the average amount of its notes in circulation,— such circulation to be ascertained in such manner as the Minister of Finance and Receiver General decides; and his decision shall be final : (New.)

9. In the event of the winding up the business of a bank by reason of insolvency or otherwise, the Treasury Board may, on the application of the directors, or of the liquidator, receiver, assignee or other proper official, and on being satisfied that proper arrangements have been made for the payment of the notes of the bank and any interest thereon, pay over to such directors, liquidator, receiver, assignee or other proper official, the amount at the credit of the bank, or such portion thereof as it thinks expedient : (New.)

Repayment of amount if bank is wound up.

Treasury Board may regulate management of fund.

10. The Treasury Board may make all such rules and regulations as it thinks expedient with reference to the payment of any moneys out of the said fund, and the manner, place and time of such payments, the collection of all amounts due to the said fund, all accounts to be kept in connection therewith, and generally the management of the said fund and all matters relating thereto : (New.)

Enforcement of payment.

11. The Minister of Finance and Receiver General may, in his official name, by action in the Exchequer Court of Canada enforce payment (with costs of action) of any sum due and payable by any bank under the provisions of this section. (New.)

All the provisions of this section are new. They provide for the formation of a safety fund, called "The Bank Circulation Redemption Fund," created for the purpose of ensuring the speedy redemption of the notes of any insolvent bank bonâ fide in circulation at the time of the suspension of payment by such bank.

Notes of bank to be payable at par throughout Canada.

55. The bank shall make such arrangements as are necessary to ensure the circulation at par in any and every part of Canada of all notes issued or re-issued by it and intended for circulation ; and towards this purpose the bank shall establish agencies for the redemption and payment of its notes at the cities of Halifax, St. John, Charlottetown, Montreal, Toronto, Winnipeg and Victoria, and at such other places as are, from time to time, designated by the Treasury Board. (New.)

56. The bank shall always receive in payment its own notes at par at any of its offices, and whether they are made payable there or not: (R.S.C. cap. 120, sec. 41, part.)

Redemption o notes.

2. The chief place of business of the bank shall always be one of the places at which its notes are made payable. (R.S.C. cap. 120, sec. 41, ss. 2.)

Payable at chief place of business.

57. The bank, when making any payment, shall, on the request of the person to whom the payment is to be made, pay the same, or such part thereof. not exceeding one hundred dollars, as such person requests, in Dominion notes for one, two or four dollars each, at the option of such person: Provided always, that no payment, whether in Dominion notes or bank notes, shall be made in bills that are torn or partially defaced by excessive handling. (R.S C. cap. 120, sec. 42, with proviso added.)

Payments in Dominion notes.

Torn or defaced notes.

58. The bonds, obligations and bills, obligatory or of credit, of the bank under its corporate seal, and signed by the president or vice-president and countersigned by a cashier or assistant cashier, which are made payable to any person, shall be assignable by endorsement thereon; and bills or notes of the bank signed by the president, vice-president, cashier or other officer appointed by the directors of the bank to sign the same, promising the pay-

Bonds. notes &c., how and by whom to be signed.

ment of money to any person or to his order, or
to the bearer, though not under the corporate
seal of the bank, shall be binding and obligatory on it in like manner and with the like
force and effect as they would be upon any
private person, if issued by him in his private
or natural capacity, and shall be assignable in
like manner as if they were so issued by a
private person in his natural capacity : Provided always, that the directors of the bank
may, from time to time, authorize, or depute any
cashier, assistant cashier or officer of the bank,
or any director other than the president or
vice-president, or any cashier, manager or local
director of any branch or office of discount and
deposit of the bank, to sign the notes of the
bank intended for circulation. (R.S.C. cap.
120, sec. 43.)

Proviso:
power may be
deputed to
officer.

Notes may be
signed by
machinery.

59. All bank notes and bills of the bank
whereon the name of any person intrusted or
authorized to sign such notes or bills on behalf
of the bank is impressed by machinery provided
for that purpose, by or with the authority of
the bank shall be good and valid to all intents
and purposes as if such notes and bills had been
subscribed in the proper handwriting of the
person intrusted or authorized by the bank to
sign the same respectively, and shall be bank
notes and bills within the meaning of all laws
and statutes whatever, and may be described as
bank notes or bills in all indictments and civil

or criminal proceedings whatsoever : Provided
always, that at least one signature to each note _{One signature must be written.}
or bill must be in the actual handwriting of a
person authorized to sign such note or bill.
(R.S.C. cap. 120, sec. 44, with proviso added.)

60. Every person, except a bank to which _{Penalty for un authorized issue of notes for circulation}
this Act applies, who issues or re-issues, makes,
draws, or indorses any bill, bond, note, cheque
or other instrument, intended to circulate as
money, or to be used as a substitute for money,
for any amount whatsoever, shall incur a penalty of four hundred dollars, which shall be recoverable with costs, in any court of competent
jurisdiction, by any person who sues for the
same ; and a moiety of such penalty shall belong
to the person suing for same, and the other
moiety to Her Majesty for the public uses of
Canada. (R.S.C. cap 120, sec. 83, ss. 1.)

This section is intended to secure to Banks and the Government the exclusive privilege of issuing and circulating
bank notes as money.

2. The intention to pass any such instrument _{What hall be deemed such notes.}
as money shall be presumed, if it is made for
the payment of a less sum than twenty
dollars, and is payable either in form or in fact
to the bearer thereof, or at sight, or on demand.
or at less than thirty days thereafter, or is overdue, or is in any way calculated or designed for
circulation, or as a substitute for money ; unless
such instrument is a cheque on some chartered

bank paid by the maker directly to his immediate creditor, or a promissory note, bill of exchange, bond or other undertaking for the payment of money, paid or delivered by the maker thereof to his immediate creditor, and is not designed to circulate as money or as a substitute for money. (R.S.C. cap. 120, sec. 83, ss. 2.)

61. Every person who in any way defaces any Dominion or Provincial note or bank note, whether by writing, printing, drawing or stamping thereon, or by attaching or affixing thereto, anything in the nature or form of an advertisement, shall be liable to a penalty not exceeding twenty dollars. (New.)

Defacement of notes.

Penalty.

62. Every officer charged with the receipt or disbursement of public moneys, and every officer of any bank, and every person acting as or employed by any banker, shall stamp or write in plain letters the word "counterfeit," "altered" or "worthless," upon every counterfeit or fraudulent note issued in the form of a Dominion or bank note, and intended to circulate as money, which is presented to him at his place of business; and if such officer or person wrongfully stamps any genuine note he shall, upon presentation, redeem it at the face value thereof. (New. Taken from the Criminal Law, 50 and 51 Vict., cap. 47, sec. 1.)

Counterfeit and fraudulent notes to be stamped as such.

63. Every person who designs, engraves, prints or in any manner makes, executes, utters, issues, distributes, circulates or uses any business or professional card, notice, placard, circular, hand-bill or advertisement in the likeness or similitude of any Dominion or bank note, or any obligation or security of any Government, or of any bank, is liable to a penalty of one hundred dollars or to three months' imprisonment, or to both. (New.—Taken from the Criminal Law, 50 and 51 Vict , cap. 47, sec. 2, slightly changed.) *No advertisement, &c., to be issued in the form of a note.*

BUSINESS AND POWERS OF THE BANK.

64. (*a*) The bank may open branches, agencies and offices, and may engage in and carry on business as a dealer in gold and silver coin and bullion, and it may deal in, discount, and lend money and make advances upon the security of, and may take as collateral security for any loan made by it, bills of exchange, promissory notes and other negotiable securities, or the stock, bonds, debentures and obligations of municipal and other corporations, whether secured by mortgage or otherwise, or Dominion, Provincial, British, foreign and other public securities, and it may engage in and carry on such business generally as appertains to the business of banking; (*b*) but, except as authorized by this Act, it shall not, either directly or indirectly, deal *Branches and agencies. General powers of bank. Certain business may not be transacted by the bank.*

in the buying, or selling, or bartering of goods, wares and merchandise. or engage or be engaged in any trade or business whatsoever; and it shall not, either directly or indirectly, purchase, or deal in, or lend money, or make advances upon the security or pledge of any share of its own capital stock, or of the capital stock of any bank; and it shall not, either directly or indirectly, lend money or make advances upon the security, mortgage, or hypothecation of any land, tenements, or immovable property, or of any ships or other vessels, or upon the security of any goods, wares and merchandise.

(*a.*) This section is a combination with some changes of several sections and parts of sections of the Repealed Act R.S.C. Cap. 120, viz: sections 45, 46, 59 and 60.

POWERS OF THE BANK.

The first part of the section, after giving power to open branches, agencies and offices, expressly authorizes the bank (1) to carry on business as a dealer in gold and silver coin and bullion:

(2) To deal in
(3) To discount
(4) To lend money and make advances upon the security of
(5) And to take as collateral security for any loan made by it

Bills of Exchange and Promissory Notes and other negotiable securities or the stock, bonds, debentures and obligations of municipal and other Corporations whether secured by mortgage or otherwise, or Dominion, Provincial, British, Foreign and other public securities.

(6) and to engage in and carry on such business as generally appertains to the business of banking.

The previous acts did not in express and positive terms confer many of the above powers on banks, but banks were nevertheless held to have some of them by implication. For example in the case of Jones vs. The Imperial Bank, 23 Gr. 269 (1876) an attempt was made, by means of an injunction, to prevent the Imperial Bank from purchasing, from the Water Commissioners of the City of Toronto, certain debentures of the City of Toronto. It was contended, by the applicants for the injunction, that section 60 of R.S.C. c. 120, by implication, gave power to the bank only to lend money on this class of debentures, that there was no express power to purchase such debentures and by implication, arising from the provisions of said section 60, the bank was prevented from purchasing as distinguished from lending money upon the same. Mr. Justice Proudfoot, however, after discussing very fully the meaning of the word "discount," and citing several authorities giving definitions of it, held that the dealing in bonds was covered by the words *of exception* contained in section 45 of the same statute, viz : " except as a "dealer in . . . Bills of Exchange, discounting of Pro- "missory Notes and negotiable securities and in such trade "generally as appertains to the business of banking ;" at page 274, he thus summarizes his opinion,—" The con- " clusion which seems to me deducible from these " acts is that the business of banking consists in dealing in " money, the precious metals, and in bonds and negotiable " securities ; that this dealing confers the power of lending on "them or of purchasing them, whichever the bank directors " may deem most for the advantage of the corporation and " that whether to buy cr lend is a matter of internal manage- " ment which the directors may determine ;" and at page 270 he says : " To discount a negotiable security is to buy " it at a discount or . . . . . to lend money on " its security."

See also Grant on banking (1884) p. 291, where it is laid down that " where a banker discounts a bill for a customer, giving him credit for the amount of the bill and debiting him with the discount, there is a complete purchase of the bill by the banker in whom the whole property and interest vest as much as in any chattel he possesses. A banker discounting a bill, whether for a customer or a stranger, there being no indorsement by the customer or stranger and the bill not being given in payment of an ante-cedent debt, is a mere purchaser and on the bankruptcy of the acceptor has no recourse against the party from whom he took it."

By the present act the powers of the bank do not rest on implication but are conferred in express terms. The bank is authorized expressly " to deal in " the securities mentioned in clause 64. This would clearly authorize the bank to buy or sell any of such securities. It must be noticed that power is also given, as well to make advances and lend money upon such securities, as to take them as security for past loans. The bank cannot, however, lend money on the ordinary bank notes, see sec. 52.

As to what comes within the definition of the business of banking—See Abbott's Dig. Corp. p. 56 and Quirt vs. Queen 19 S.C.R. 510 (1891) and the cases there referred to.

LIMITATIONS ON THE POWER OF THE BANK.

(*b*) The second part of section 64 commencing with the words, " but except as authorized by this Act,"—is in restric-tion of the powers of the bank.

It is conceived that the words " *except as authorized by this act* " are intended to be read before the words, " it shall not," wherever they subsequently occur in this section.

Assuming this construction to be correct then :—

Firstly :—a bank is forbidden, *except as authorized by this act* " either directly or indirectly to deal in the buying or " selling or bartering of goods, wares and merchandise or en-" gage or be engaged in any trade or business whatsoever.'

It is to be observed, that by this part of the clause, banks are prohibited only *from dealing in* the buying or selling or bartering of goods, wares or merchandise, it would therefore seem most probable that banks may, owing to special cir-cumstances or for reasons which could not have been fore-seen or anticipated, acquire and sell, or dispose of goods, wares or merchandise and for that purpose engage to some extent in business other than banking.   Thus, if a bank were to acquire a valid security, say on a mill and a stock of lumber and logs, and [afterwards, owing to the inability of the debtor to pay his indebtedness, were to duly obtain an absolute title to the property, it seems to us that the bank could, under such circumstances, proceed to sell the lumber and to convert the saw logs into lumber, if that would make them more valuable for sale, and for this purpose to work the mill. This appears to be the result of the English and American authorities on the subject.   See Sacketts Head Bank vs: Lewis Bank, 11 'Barb., 43. Brice on Ultra Vires, p. 210.

In Quebec, too, it has been held in the Molson's Bank vs. Kennedy, 10 R.L. 110 (1879), that where a bank wishing to guarantee a purchase of goods telegraphs to the sellers— "If you send to the M. Bank, Montreal, goods to the amount of £——— purchased by K & Co. about July 1st, sending us the bills of lading and documents in time, we will guarantee the collection,"—the bank does not thereby violate the provisions of the Banking Act.

In Radford vs. the Merchant's Bank of Canada, 3 Ont. R. 529 (1883), the facts were as follows : The Agent of the Merchant's Bank at Kingston represented to the plaintiff that the defendants had purchased the business of one A, a manufacturer of horse power machines, and were manufacturing horse power machines of A's make, and had them for sale, and that he recommended them highly.   The plaintiff purchased a machine, and subsequently brought an action against the bank for breach of warranty on the sale of this machine.   It appeared in the evidence that A was a debtor of the bank, and having become insolvent, the bank had acquired the machines from his assignee. The case was decided on two grounds, but both the judges who decided it expressed the opinion that the bank, being expressly prohibited from buying and selling goods, could not be bound by any warranty, express or implied on their sale.   It is true that in this case the bank had improperly acquired the machines (section 69 not authorizing the purchase) and the decision may have been based on that fact ; but, if the machines had been properly acquired say,—by a legal and valid mortgage to the bank and thereafter by the extinguishment of the equity of redemption by release under section 70—surely the bank could then sell and dispose of the machines, and if so, why could not it give a warranty on their sale if that would be the most advantageous course to pursue,—see also Exchange Bank vs. Fletcher 19, S.C.R. 278, (1891).

Secondly :—a bank is forbidden, *except as authorized by this act*, " either directly or indirectly to purchase, deal in or lend " money or make advances upon the security or pledge of " any share of its own stock or of the stock of any other " bank." This will set at rest all doubt as to the existence of a prohibition in the previous acts against lending money on the stock of other banks [see per Patterson J. in Exchange Bank vs. Fletcher, 19 S.C.R. at p. 284, (1891)]. In the last named case the court held that the prohibition to lend money on the shares of other banks only applied to the bank lending the money—and not to the borrower of the money who gave the shares as security, so that on payment of the loan the bank was bound to return the shares or pay their value to the borrower, and this case would still seem to be law under the present Act.

Although a bank is prohibited from lending money on its own shares it is given a lien thereon for all debts owing by a shareholder ; see sections 35, 38 and 65.

Thirdly :—a bank is forbidden, *except as authorized by this act*, " either directly or indirectly to lend money or make ad- " vances upon the security, mortgage or hypothecation of any " land or tenements or immoveable property or of any ships " or other vessels or of any goods, wares or merchandise."

For the exceptions to the above prohibitions see the subsequent clauses of this act from 68 to 79 inclusive.

The general policy of clause 64, no doubt, is to compel banks to carry on a proper and legitimate banking business and to keep the capital of the banks flowing in the daily channels of commerce and to deter them from locking up their money by lending it or investing it in real estate, or other classes of property which are not easily convertible into cash.

For an infraction of the provisions of this section a penalty is imposed on the banks by section 79. Supposing a bank enters into a forbidden transaction, lends money on the security of a mortgage on real estate for example, how does the statute affect such a transaction? Does it merely subject the bank to a penalty and perhaps its charter to possible forfeiture or does it go further still and also avoid the mortgage security—or further still and also make the contract of loan illegal so as to be irrecoverable by the bank?

In a recent case on the subject it has been held, that it not only exposes the bank to the penalty, but also avoids the transaction.

" This prohibition is a law of public policy in the public interest and any transaction in violation thereof is necessarily null and void. No court can be called on to give effect to any such transaction, or to enforce any contract or security on which money is lent, or advances, as thus prohibited, are made," per Ritchie, C. J., in Bank of Toronto vs. Perkins, 8 S.C.R., 610 (1883).

In the above extract, the Chief Justice, if correctly reported, seems to us to go too far. His judgment would seem to imply not only that the mortgage was void, but that the advance which it was given to secure created no valid debt. The other judges who expressed opinions did not go so far. Strong, J., at page 611 of the report says : " All we have to decide is whether a bank making an advance or loan of money on a mortgage of real property in violation of the prohibition contained in the section referred to is notwithstanding entitled to the benefit of the security."

In the case of Exchange Bank vs. Fletcher, 19 S C.R. 278, (1891), it was apparently held that a prohibited transaction was only avoided as against the bank. That a man who had transferred to the bank shares in another bank as security for a debt could on payment of the debt come into a Court of Justice and demand the return of the shares or the value thereof.

There are two cases in the Privy Council both of which
are referred to in the Bank of Toronto vs. Perkins, above
cited, in which the construction of Bank Charters containing
similar prohibitory clauses was much discussed.   In the first
case, the National Bank of Australasia vs. Cherry, L.R., 3
P.C., 299 (1870), Lord Cairns in delivering judgment at p. 307,
says : " It appears, therefore, to their lordships that there
are considerations of public policy involved in this clause,
but it is also true to say, that those considerations of public
policy look to and deal with the management of the bank,
and have for their object the limitation of the powers and
authority of the bank."

" That being so, and without for the present turning to the
facts of this particular case, it would seem to have been the
object of the Legislature in this clause, not to make void
the contracts for such advances as between the bank and
their customers, in the same way that in former times contracts
open to the objections of the usury laws were made void,
but rather to make it something ultra vires the bank to take,
upon the occasion of contracts for those advances, securities of the kind mentioned in this section.   And this construction of the section would harmonize with what was very
properly, as their lordships think, admitted at the bar on behalf of the respondeuts—that upon a transaction of the
kind described, the contract for the loan of money would be
perfectly valid, and the question would be confined to a
question as to whether the bank had the power to take the
security which it took for the advance ....
At the time of the advance, and as part of the
contract of advance, the bank was not to be at .
liberty to stipulate for, or to obtain, landed or mercantile
security.   *That is the construction contended for by the Re-
spondents, and their Lordships, at all events for the purpose of
argument, will assume that it is the proper construction.*   On
the other hand, if there should be an advance made, and a
debt incurred and due from the customer to the bank, the
bank was to be at liberty to take security for that *overdue advance*, either in the shape of land or in the shape of
merchandise as described in the Act."

In the second case, Ayers vs. The South Australian Banking Co., L.R. 3 P.C., 548, (1871), Lord Justice Mellish in the course of delivering the judgment of the Privy Council and in answer to the argument founded on a clause in the charter declaring that it shall not be lawful for the bank to make advances on merchandise says at p. 559: "There may be also question whether, under any circumstances, the effect of violating such a provision is more than this, the Crown may take advantage of it as a forfeiture of the charter, but the only point which it appears to their Lordships is necessary to be determined in the present case is this, that whatever effect such a clause may have, it does not prevent property passing, either in goods or in lands, under a conveyance or instrument which, under the ordinary circumstances of law, would pass it..... Their Lordships are of opinion, that whatever other effect it has, it cannot have the effect of preventing the property passing. If that were otherwise, the consequences might be most lamentable, because if the property never passed to them, they could not themselves convey any property to third persons. Transactions of the most honest description might be set aside. They might do what is a very common thing, make advances and take Bills of Exchange with the Bills of Lading attached. If it is to be said that the property in the goods mentioned in the Bill of Lading does not pass to them, then any purchaser to whom they might sell the goods under the Bill of Lading would get no title, and the original owner who had received the full proceeds of the goods, or a large advance upon them, might say, 'Oh, the property never passed to the South Australian Bank, and therefore it never passed to you.' Counsel for the appellants admitted that he could find no authority for the proposition, that any violation of such a condition of a charter would prevent the property in goods passing to the person to whom an instrument otherwise valid professed to pass it, and their Lordships are of opinion, that whatever effect the violation of such a condition may have, it has not the effect of preventing the property in the goods passing, or of preventing an action of Trover being maintained if there is a wrongful conversion."

—See also Bank of New South Wales vs. Campbell L.R. 11 App. Cases 192 (1886).

It has been decided here, and in the United States, that if a mortgage of lands be given to a bank to secure indebtedness previously incurred, and also advances then made on the security of such mortgage, such mortgage is not void in toto, but constitutes a good and valid security to the bank to the extent of the pre-existing indebtedness, if the amount thereof can be clearly shewn.   See the following cases—

Commercial Bank vs. Bank of U. C. 7 Gr. 430 (1859).

Kansas Valley National Bank vs. Powell, 2 Dill. C.C. 371.

Allen vs. First National Bank of Xenia, 23 Ohio St. R. 97.

It has also been decided in the National Bank of Australasia vs. Cherry, above cited, and also in the Commercial Bank vs. Bank of Upper Canada, above cited, that though the taking by the bank of a mortgage on real estate, to secure an advance made on such security, would be ultra vires and invalid, the advance itself would create a valid debt and consequently, the bank could acquire a valid charge on the same property, to secure re-payment of the same debt, by a mortgage subsequently given by the debtor to the bank ; accord also, Grant vs. La Banque Nationale, 9 O.R. 411, (1885).   It does not seem to us, that the law is quite settled yet, in regard to the consequences of an infraction by the bank of the provisions of this act in relation to taking securities.   At present the law in Canada appears to be, that the act not only imposes a penalty on the bank for lending money or making advances upon the security of real estate, &c., but also renders invalid the security so taken.   We do not think any thing further than this has been decided.

EFFECT OF TRAFFICKING IN SHARES ON THE LIABILITY OF A SHAREHOLDER.

In the winding up of the Central Bank, some shareholders objected to be placed on the list of contributories, on the ground that the bank had been trafficking in its own shares, and that the shares in question had been acquired in the course of such traffic and transferred to the cashier of the bank, in trust for the bank, by and through whom they had been transferred to or acquired by the contributories. Held, assuming these facts to be true, that though this might give the contributories a right to rescind, during the currency of the banking institution, they were of no moment after the rights of creditors represented by the liquidators arose. The matter was not an absolute nullity, but at most, one which the shareholders could waive as voidable, and it became, by the suspension, of unimpeachable validity as between these contributories and the liquidators. In the matter of the Central Bank of Canada, Baine's case—Nasmith's case—16 Ontario Reports 293, (1888), 16 Ont. App. R. 237, (1889), 18 Ont. App. R. 209 (1891).

A shareholder having been placed on the list of contributories, in the winding up proceedings of the Central Bank, in respect of certain shares owned by him at the time of the suspension of the bank, appealed on the ground that the transfer of his shares was a fraudulent transaction, since, in violation of the provisions of the bank act R.C.S., cap 120, sec. 45 (now sec. 64), the bank had been trafficking in its own shares, for the purpose of keeping up the appearance of *bona fide* sales and so increasing the market price of its shares, and had taken the appellant's promissory notes in payment for his shares, undertaking not to enforce such notes, but to deliver them up upon a re-sale of the shares being effected, which transactions were ultra vires of the bank. Held, that this was no defence as against the liquidators, who represented the creditors as well as the bank. Re Central Bank—J. D. Henderson's case, 17 O.R. 110 (1889).

"Goods, wares and merchandise"—for the meaning of these words, see sec. 2, ss. 3, and the notes to sec. 73.

65. The bank shall have a privileged lien, for any debt or liability for any debt to the bank, on the shares of its own capital stock and on any unpaid dividends of the debtor or person liable, and may decline to allow any transfer of the shares of such debtor or person until such

Bank to have lien on debtor's shares.

Sale of such shares.

debt is paid; and the bank shall, within twelve months after such debt has accrued and become payable, sell such shares, and notice shall be given to the holder thereof of the intention of

Notice.

the bank to sell the same, by mailing such notice in the post office to the last known address of such holder, at least thirty days prior to such sale; and upon such sale being made the president, vice-president, manager or cashier shall

Transfer in case of sale.

execute a transfer of such shares to the purchaser thereof in the usual transfer book of the bank, which transfer shall vest in such purchaser all the rights in or to such shares which were possessed by the holder thereof, with the same obligation of warranty on his part as if he were the vendor thereof, but without any warranty from the bank or by the officer of the bank executing such transfer. (R.S.C. cap. 120, sec. 59, changed).

This section now makes it the duty of the bank to sell the shares on which it is given a lien within 12 months after the debt, secured by such lien, has become payable—otherwise the section is substantially the same as it was in the repealed act.

In the case of Cook vs. Royal Canadian Bank, 20 Gr., 1 (1873), it was held under the law as it then stood, that the bank had a lien on the stock of any debtor for overdue debts, and could refuse to allow a transfer of such stock until such overdue debts were paid. At page 12, Vice-Chancellor Blake uses the following language : " I am of opinion that a statement by the bank of the amount for which stock is held on account of past due liabilities, without any further representation, or any agreement in respect thereof, does not bind it at a future day to accept such sum where other liabilities incurred at the time the inquiry was made, have meanwhile matured and remain unpaid."

Since this judgment was delivered sections 19 and 51 of 34 Vic., c. 5, have been repealed and new sections, from time to time, substituted therefor, and a clause has been added to what is now section 45. The sections which now deal with the question of the bank's lien are sections 35, 38 and 65 and from their language we think that they give the bank a lien for all debts owing to it, as well those "*owing and payable*," as those "*owing but not payable.*" This present section now provides that the bank shall have a privileged lien for any debt or liability for any debt to the bank, (not saying as the repealed section of 34 Vict., cap. 5, sec. 51, did "for any overdue debt"), and may decline to allow any transfer of shares till such debt is paid. Having regard therefore to this change of language, we are inclined to think that the bank, under the present act, has a lien on the stock of a debtor for all current as well as matured debts. See on this point Stockton vs. Malleable Iron Co., I.R. 2 Ch Div. 101 (1875). See also Reese vs. The Bank of Commerce, 14 Md. 271. Angell & Amos on Corporations (1882) secs. 571-574.

In addition to the above lien the banker, by the common law, would, it is conceived, have a general lien for the general balance due by the customer on all bills and negotiable instruments and perhaps other securities handed by the customer to the banker generally; that is, without specific appropriation, for the purpose of being realized or collected and the proceeds carried into the account of the customer. The lien does not extend to securities handed to the banker for safe-keeping or for the purpose of being dealt with in a specific manner. See Walker on Banking Law p. 185.

66. The stock, bonds, debentures or securities, acquired and held by the bank as collateral security, may, in case of default to pay the debt, for securing which they were so acquired and held, be dealt with, sold and conveyed either

Collateral securities may be similarly dealt with.

in like manner and subject to the same restrictions as are herein provided in respect of stock of the bank on which it has acquired a lien under this Act, or in like manner as and subject to the restrictions under which a private individual might in like circumstances deal with, sell and convey the same, but without obligation to sell the same within twelve months: (R.S.C. cap. 120, sec. 60, ss. 2, in part with addition.)

All the words of this section after the words " this Act " are new. They give additional powers of sale to the bank. By the law of England if personal property is pledged to secure a debt payable at a fixed time, if the debt is not paid at such time then the pledgee has a right to sell the property pledged in order to have his debt. If there is no time fixed for the payment of the debt the pledgee has a right upon request to insist upon prompt payment thereof, and in default thereof the pledgee upon reasonable demand and notice to pledgor may sell the property pledged for the purpose of satisfying the debt. (as to sale of Stock see S. 65)

Right to do so may be waived. 2. The right so to deal with and dispose of such stock, bonds, debentures or securities in manner aforesaid may be waived or varied by any agreement between the bank and the owner of such stock, bonds, debentures or securities, made at the time at which such debt was incurred, or if the time of payment of such debt has been extended, then by an agreement made at the time of such extension. (R S.C. cap. 120, sec. 60, ss. 2 part.)

67. The bank may acquire and hold real and immovable property for its actual use and occupation and the management of its business, and may sell or dispose of the same, and acquire other property in its stead for the same purpose. (R.S.C. cap. 120, sec. 47.)

Real estate for occupation.

68. The bank may take, hold and dispose of mortgages and *hypothèques* upon real or personal, immovable or movable property, by way of additional security for debts contracted to the bank in the course of its business; and the rights, powers and privileges which the bank is by this Act declared to have or to have had in respect of real or immovable property mortgaged to it, shall be held and possessed by it in respect of any personal or movable property which is mortgaged or hypothecated to it. (R.S.C. cap. 120, sec. 48 with slight additions).

Mortgages as additional security.

The only change in this section is the addition of the words "immovable and movable" wherever they occur therein.

Section 64 in substance enacts that the bank shall not "except as authorized by this Act," either directly or indirectly, lend money or make advances upon the security or mortgage of lands, or of goods, wares or merchandize.

The present section, therefore, is one of the enabling sections referred to in section 64 and authorizes the bank to acquire security on real and personal property under the limitations herein imposed.

MORTGAGES MAY BE TAKEN FOR " DEBTS CONTRACTED."

It will be observed that the bank is authorized to take and hold mortgages on real or personal property only *by way of additional security* for "*debts contracted* to the bank, *in the course of its business.*"

Supposing a bank agrees to discount a note, can it take security for the debt thereby contracted co-temporaneously with the discount of the note? Opinions have been expressed that if the bank really advances money on the security of a note or bill (and this is a question of fact to be determined on a consideration of all the circumstances of each case), it may co-temporaneously with such advance validly take a mortgage as collateral security to secure repayment thereof. Whenever this is done, however, it will always be a question of fact, whether the money was not really advanced on the mortgage and the note created merely to give color and lend the appearance of legality to the transaction. It would, therefore, be extremely dangerous for a bank to make an advance on negotiable paper and at the same time take a mortgage as collateral security for repayment thereof. There are numerous cases on this section. Only two will be cited at any length, as they really appear to contain a full exposition of the proper interpretation of the clause.

In the Commercial Bank vs. Bank of U.C., 7 Gr., 430, decided in 1859 (and in the court below, 7 Gr. 250) Chief Justice Robinson, at page 430, thus discusses the question now under consideration : "It is quite true that whenever the money is advanced, whether it be just before or at the time of making the mortgage, then there is literally a debt due but not a debt contracted in the course of the business of the bank—that is, of its legitimate and proper business, which the *lending money upon mortgage* of real property certainly cannot be, until the statutes are repealed or altered. When it is shewn that the mortgage in any case was taken by a bank 'as an additional *security* for a debt contracted to it in the course of its business,' then the question occurs whether that can only be taken to mean a debt that had been *previously* incurred with it in the course of its business, or whether a mortgage may not be taken as additional security for a debt that had no previous existence, but which the bank were about to allow a party to contract, by advancing him money at that time, in the proper course of their business ; as, for instance, if any merchant had brought to the bank, on the 21st of May, 1855, for discount, a bill drawn by Henry Bull, jr., on Bull Brothers, and accepted by the latter, could the bank properly have taken a mortgage from either party to the bill, or from the person who brought it and got the money, to secure them the money which they advanced upon the bill ?   That is not this case, and I shall only therefore say, that, as the words of the statute are not against it, so I think it might, *perhaps*, be held that the spirit and intention of the Act are not opposed to it ; and that a mortgage so taken might be upheld, when it appears that the mortgage was really and in truth taken to secure the transaction upon the bill, and not that the bill was created for the mere purpose of upholding and giving color to the mortgage. That would be a question of fact, upon which the conclusion that a jury might come to would be in general so uncertain that I dare say the banks will not think it prudent to risk their money on a real security in any such case, where the nature of the transaction might appear to be at all equivocal —so long, I mean, as the present statutes continue in force." In the case of the Royal Canadian Bank vs. Cummer, 15 Gr., p. 627 (decided in 1869), the late Chief Justice Sprague (then Vice-Chancellor) in his judgment said, at p. 631 : "take the simple fact of deposit by way of security by the debtor of a bank, to a bank, there being a debt, and there being further advances contemplated but not yet made, a deposit for the debt due would be lawful ; but a deposit by way of security, against which the bank customer might draw, would be against the law ; and the law upon this point is so well known to bankers that they would hardly be likely to transgress it."

In the Bank of Toronto vs. Perkins, 8 S.C.R. 603 (decided in 1883), Chief Justice Ritchie in his opinion uses the following language : " I agree with Chief Justice Dorion that the transfer made to the appellants of a mortgage to secure an advance on a promissory note discounted at the same time that the transfer was made, was on the part of the bank in violation of the Banking Act, a clumsy attempt at evasion of the 34th Vic., ch. 5, sec. 40, which enacts that ' the bank shall not, either directly or indirectly, lend money

or make advances upon the security, mortgage or hypothecation of any lands and tenements.'"

Strong, J., in his opinion in the same case uses the following language : "We must therefore take the transaction to
have been a mortgage given, not to secure a past debt, but
to cover a contemporaneous loan, and therefore void under
the statute."

Gwynne, J., after citing Chief Justice Robinson's opinion
above given in the case of the Commercial Bank vs. Bank of
Upper Canada, proceeds as follows : "Now, I do not desire
to call in question any part of the opinion of the learned
Chief Justice as here expressed as to the validity of a mortgage *bona fide* given or assigned to a bank by way of collateral security for an advance made by the bank upon regular
business paper, or in the ordinary course of their business as
bankers, concurrently with the giving or assigning to them of
a mortgage upon lands as additional security, or to express
any opinion upon that point, inasmuch as sitting here as a
juror, and having the duty imposed upon me of finding the
facts in the case, I have been unable to bring my mind to
the conclusion that this is such a case; on the contrary, the
conviction formed in my mind by the facts is that the transaction between Bunnell and the bank, of the 19th January,
1876, was primarily based upon the security of the mortgages
upon real estate assigned to the bank by the deed of that
date.   That the note for $26,000 recited in that deed had
not then been, if ever it was, in fact, discounted or agreed to
be discounted as an ordinary banking transaction.   A note
made by one payable to his own order twelve months after
date is not ordinary business paper ; that the note did not
then constitute any debt due from Bunnell to the bank, that
it was not made for the purpose of being discounted by them
in the ordinary course of their business as bankers, but was
given existence for the mere purpose of upholding and giving
color to the assignment of the mortgages, the whole having
been assigned, and contrived for the purpose of evading the
statute, and the mortgages were not assigned really and in
truth to secure an independent banking transaction on the
note. . .   . Upon the whole, therefore, as I have

said, I can come to no other conclusion than that the note was given existence for the sole purpose of upholding and giving color to the mortgage and its transfer, which latter contained a false recital of a debt due for the purpose of eluding a discovery of the true nature of the transaction."

The meaning of the words "debts contracted" was very much considered and discussed by Mr. Justice Story in the case of Carver v. Braintree, 2 Story, C.C., at page 448. He thought it was not a violent construction of the statute to read these words as equivalent to "liabilities incurred." In the French law the terms debtor and creditor are applied to the parties who contract any species of obligation. Pothier, vol. 1, p. 74.

AS TO THE PRESUMPTION IN FAVOR OF VALIDITY OF A TRANSACTION.

In the case of The Royal Canadian Bank v. Cummer, 15 Gr., 627 (1869), there being a doubt whether the mortgage in question was intended to secure future advances *only*, or to secure all past indebtedness as well as future advances, —the court decided in favor of the bank, on the ground that where there is a doubt the presumption should be that the transaction was in conformity with the statute, and so legal, the maxim being *omnia presummunter rite esse acta*.

AS TO THE APPLICATION OF PAYMENTS WHERE MORTGAGES ARE INTENDED AS CONTINUING SECURITY, &C., AND AS TO THE EFFECT ON THE SECURITY OF THE RENEWAL OF THE PAPER REPRESENTING THE IN- DEBTEDNESS.

As to the construction of mortgages given under this section, as a continuing security to secure an indebtedness, where the indebtedness has been changed but not reduced in amount, see Cameron v. Kerr, 3 Ont. App. R. 30 (1878). In this case, after the mortgage was given the mortgagors' line of discount was increased, but no separate account of the liabilities secured by the mortgage and the further advances was kept, the proceeds of the discounts and cash

deposits being carried to the mortgagors' credit in one open
current account, against which they drew cheques and retired
the notes secured by the mortgage as they matured. The
mortgagors became insolvent on the 12th August, 1875,
their indebtedness in the meantime never having been
really reduced below the amount of the mortgage debt.
Held, affirming the judgment of Blake, V.C., that
this mode of keeping the accounts had not operated as
a discharge of the mortgage debt. See also Merchant's
Bank v. Moffatt, 5 Ont. R., 122 (1883) and 11 S.C.R., 46
(1885). In Dominion Bank v. Oliver, 17 Ont. R., 402
(1889) it was held by Chancellor Boyd that "Where a bank,
holding a mortgage as additional security for the payment of
certain notes, substitutes for these notes renewals from time
to time, without, however, receiving actual payment, the
whole series of notes and renewals form links in one and the
same chain of liability, which is secured by the mortgage,
although, as a matter of book-keeping the bank may have
treated the first notes, and the subsequent substituted notes
as paid by the application of the proceeds, from time to time,
of the renewals."

RIGHTS AND POWERS OF BANK OVER PERSONAL PROPERTY MORTGAGED TO IT.

By this section the bank is declared to have the same
rights, powers and privileges in respect of " personal property
mortgaged to it as it possesses in respect of real property
mortgaged or hypothecated to it." For the powers which
the bank has in respect of real property mortgaged or
hypothecated to it, see sections 70 and 71.

In Thompson v. Molsons Bank, 16 S.C.R., 664 (1889),
the Supreme Court of Canada held, that when an advance is
made on a warehouse receipt, the bank may stipulate that
any surplus moneys, arising from a sale by the bank of the
goods covered by such warehouse receipt, after payment
of such advance, may be applied in payment of other
indebtedness owing to the bank and existing at the time of
the making of such advance.

See also the following cases, and the cases therein cited, onthe construction of this section generally :   McDonell v. Bank of Upper Canada, 7 U. C. Q. B. 252 (1850).   Bank of Upper Canada v. Killaly, 21 U.C.Q.B. 9 (1861).   Bank of Montreal v. McWhirter, 17 U. C. C. P. 513 (1867). Molson's Bank v. McDonald, 2 Ont. A. R. 102 (1877), affirming S. C. 40 U. C. Q. B. 529.   Merchants' Bank v. Bostwick, 3 Ont. A.R. 24 (1878), and Grant v. La Banque Nationale, 9 Ont. R. 411 (1885), which was a case of a pledge of a timber limit in Quebec, wherein the construction of section 28 of The Quebec Timber Regulations arose.

TECHNICAL DEFECTS IN SECURITY.

Can a Liquidator under the Winding-up Act, (R.S.C., cap. 129,) or an assignee under the Ontario Act respecting assignments (R.S.O. 1887, cap. 124,) object to the want of registration or other formal defects in the security ? See in Re Rainy Lake Lumber Co., 15 Ont. App. R. 749, (1888), Burland vs. Moffat, 11 S.C.R. 76 (1885), Porteous vs. Reynar, L.R. 13 App. Cas. 120 (1887), Robinson vs. Cook, 6 Ont. R., 590 (1884), Tennant vs. Union Bank, 19 Ont. App. R. (1892).

HOLDING NOTES AS COLLATERAL SECURITY.

A bank holding notes of other persons as collateral security for a customer's debt is bound to use reasonable diligence in collecting the same, and if loss ensues the bank is liable to the customer to the extent of the loss occasioned by its want of diligence.   Ryan vs. McConnell, 18 Ont. R. 409 (1889).

BENEFIT OF SECURITY.

The bank sometimes gets the benefit of a security without expressly stipulating for it.   Thus in a recent case it appears that a tradesman sold goods to customers, taking promissory notes for the price, and also hire receipts, by which the property remained in him until full payment thereof was made, and that the notes were discounted through the medium of a third person by the Central Bank, and it further appeared that the bank was made aware, when the line of discount was opened, of the course of dealing and of the securities held, but was not put in actual possession of the securities and there was no express contract in regard to them. Nevertheless, in an action by the bank to recover the securities or their proceeds from the assignee for creditors of the tradesman, it was held, that the securities were accessory to the debt ; that in equity the transfer of the notes was a transfer of the securities ; that the defendant was in no higher position than his assignor, and could not resist the claim to have the receipts accompany the notes ; and that it was not material that the relation of assignor and assignee did not immediately exist between the tradesman and the Central Bank. Central Bank vs. Garland, 20 Ont. R. 142 (1890), 18 A. R. 438 (1891).

69. The bank may purchase any lands or real or immovable property offered for sale under execution, or in insolvency, or under the order or decree of a court, as belonging to any debtor to the bank, or offered for sale by a mortgagee or other encumbrancer having priority over a mortgage or other encumbrance held by the bank, or offered for sale by the bank under a power of sale given to it for that purpose, in cases in which, under similar circumstances, an individual could so purchase, without any restriction as to the value of the property which it may so purchase, and may acquire a title thereto as any individual purchasing at sheriff's sale, or under a power of sale, in like circumstances, could do, and may take, have, hold and dispose of the same at pleasure. (R.S.C. cap. 120, sec. 49, slightly changed and added to).

Purchase of land under execution, &c.

This section apparently enables the bank to purchase "lands or real or immovable property," (1) offered for sale under execution or (2) in insolvency or (3) under the order or decree of a court, as belonging to a debtor of the bank, or (4) offered for sale by a mortgagee or other incumbrancer having priority over a mortgage or other incumbrance held by the bank. (This power is an additional one given by this Act). (5) or offered for sale by the bank under a power of sale given to it for that purpose, in cases when, in similar circumstances, an individual could so purchase (By English law a mortgagee selling cannot purchase—he cannot occupy the antagonistic positions of seller and buyer at the same time.)

By the conjoint operation of this section, as it now reads, and sec. 68 the bank, holding an incumbrance on personal or moveable property, could purchase the same if offered for sale by a mortgagee or other incumbrancer having a prior incumbrance thereon ; the last mentioned section declaring that the rights, powers and privileges which the bank is by this Act declared to have or to have had in respect of real property mortgaged to it, shall be held or possessed by it, in respect of any personal property which is mortgaged or hypothecated to it.

70. The bank may acquire and hold an absolute title in or to real or immovable property mortgaged to it as security for a debt due or owing to it, either by obtaining a release of the equity of redemption in the mortgaged property, or by procuring a foreclosure, or by other means whereby, as between individuals, an equity of redemption can, by law, be barred, and may purchase and acquire any prior mortgage or charge on such property: Provided always, that no bank shall hold any real or immovable property, howsoever acquired, ex- *Absolute title may be acquired.* *Proviso: sale of property so acquired.*

cept such as is required for its own use, for any
period exceeding seven years from the date of
the acquisition thereof. (R S.C. cap. 120, sec.
50, slightly changed).

See also sections 69 and 71.

Banks are entitled to a decree of foreclosure upon mortgages held by them as additional security. **Bank of Upper
Canada v. Scott, 6 Chy., 451 (1858).**

It will be observed that, under this section, the power of
the bank to acquire an absolute title or to acquire a prior
charge is restricted to "real or immovable property." The
latter part of section 68, however, provides that the bank
shall have the same rights, powers and privileges in respect
of personal property, mortgaged or hypothecated to it, as by
the Act it is declared to have over real estate mortgaged to
it.

The construction of a statute of a similar character,
though not in identical language, will be found in the **Bank
of New South Wales v. Campbell, L. R. 11, App. Cas., 192,
(1886).**

WHAT IS THE EFFECT OF THE PROVISO TO ABOVE SECTION ?

The proviso is as follows :—

" Provided always, that no bank shall hold any real or im-
" movable property howsoever acquired, except such as is
" required for its own use, for any period exceeding seven
" years from the date of the acquisition thereof."

Under the English Common Law corporations had power
to take and hold lands just as natural persons had. By a
series of Statutes known as the Mortmain Acts, and which
have been held to be in force in Ontario, corporations, though
not prevented from taking lands, were forbidden from holding the same without a license in mortmain from the Crown
under pain of forfeiture of the lands (in this country) to the
Crown. As only the power of holding the lands was prohibited by these statutes, it followed that grants of land to

corporations were good so as to pass the lands to them, but so soon as such lands were taken by the corporations without a license in mortmain from the Crown, the lands became liable to be forfeited to the Crown. We do not know exactly what the law of Quebec is as to the holding of lands in mortmain by corporations. The Quebec law of mortmain was under discussion in the Chaudiere Gold Mining Company v. Desbarats, L. R. 5, P. C. 277, (1873) and it would appear from that case that the French Law of mortmain is not identical with the English.

The construction of this proviso would have to be the same in all the Provinces, for as Mr. Justice Patterson recently observed in the Enchange Bank v. Fletcher, 19 S.C.R. 288 (1891), "The Banking Act must receive the "same construction in all parts of the Dominion, what it "allows or prohibits in Quebec it must allow or prohibit in "all the other provinces. If the article (of the Code) "enunciates a rule of law peculiar to one province which "is to govern in that province the operation of this Statute, "each province may also establish a rule of interpretation to "prevail within its borders, and the uniformity of the law on "this important branch of trade and commerce, which was "to be secured by confiding it to the exclusive legislative "jurisdiction of the Dominion Parliament, will be in peril."

It is submitted that the breach of the proviso would expose the bank to the penalty prescribed by sec. 79. If the breach were *wilful and long continued* it might be regarded as an abuse of the corporate powers of the bank, and might form the foundation of proceedings for a forfeiture of the Charter. The land might also become forfeitable to the Crown, this however is doubtful and has not been decided so far as we know. We have only been able to find two cases in Ontario in which the effect of a clause of this character has been under discussion. The first is, London & Canadian Loan & Agency Co., vs. Graham, 16 Ont., R. 329 (1888), the second is, McDairmid vs. Hughes, 16 Ont., R. 570 (1888), in which the clause there in question is somewhat similar in its language to the above proviso. The statute in question in the second of these two cases, after giving the Williams Mfg. Co. power to acquire and hold lands, goes on to say, " and the company may retain the whole or any part thereof, for a period not exceeding five years.".

The Chief Justice in his judgment in this case says at page 576 :

" It seems that under these statutes an alienation in mort-
" main is voidable only, and not void, and that in this Pro-
" vince where lands are held in free and common socage,
" the lands so aliened can only be forfeited by the Crown,
" and that only after office found. See Grant on Corpora-
" tions, p. 98 ; Green's Brice's Ultra Vires, p. 12 ; Becher
" vs. Woods, 16 C.P. 29 (1865); Sheldon on Mortmain, p. 1 ;
" Hallock vs. Wilson, 7 C.P. 28 (1857) ; Brown vs. McNab,
" 20 Gr. 179 (1873) ; Vigers v. St. Paul's, 14 Q.B. 909 (1849).
" I am of opinion therefore, that the defendant cannot
" take advantage of the statutes of mortmain as against the
" alienation by Dawson to the company ; but that the Crown
" alone can take advantage of them."

Mr. Justice Street in his judgment after reviewing and discussing the statutes of mortmain proceeds as follows at page 580 :—

" The law under which the national banks in the United
" States are constituted contains a similar provision to this,
" but I have been unable to find any express decisions as to
" its effect. A somewhat similar question is discussed in Baird
" vs. The Bank of Washington, 11 Serg. & Rawle, 411, where
" the opinion is expressed that even if the grantees, who had
" taken a conveyance in satisfaction of a debt, had no right
" to hold the property conveyed, it would not therefore
" follow that the acquittance of the debt would be cancelled,
" and the land revert to the grantor, but rather that the
" rights of the parties to the conveyance, inter se, would be
" preserved, leaving to the state the right to take advantage
" of the defective title of the grantees. See also Leazure vs.
" Hillegas, 7 Serg. & Rawle, 313. This view of the law is
" approved in Morse on Banks and Banking, 3rd ed. sec. 754,
" where these cases are cited and commented upon. In my

" opinion the same consideration should govern the stipula-
" tions in this statute which limits the right of the company
" to hold for five years. The title of the company became
" defeasible by the Crown after the land had been retained
" beyond that period, and may be defeasible still on the
" ground of the limitation in the statute ;...............
" but I can find no authority for the proposition that the
" title of the company, ipso facto, terminated at the expira-
" tion of five years from the passing of the Act, or the com-
" mencement of their holding of the property ; and I am,
" therefore, of opinion that their conveyance to the plaintiff
" was effectual to pass to him the title which they held, sub-
" ject to any right of entry or defeasance which the Crown
" might possess."

If the Crown should intervene to forfeit the land, the loss
occasioned would have to be borne by the bank alone ; see
Morse on Banking, s. 74, and Baird vs. Bank of Washington,
11 Serg. & Rawle, 411.

71. Nothing in any charter, Act or law shall
be construed as ever having prevented or as
preventing the bank from acquiring and holding an absolute title to and in any such mortgaged
real or immovable property, whatever the value
thereof is, or from exercising or acting upon
any power of sale contained in any mortgage
given to it or held by it, authorizing or enabling
it to sell or convey away any property so
mortgaged. (R.S.C. cap. 120 s. 51, changed
slightly.)

Title to lands so acquired ; power of sale, &c.

See also section 70.

Section 70 expressly authorizes the bank to get in the title
to mortgaged land and immovables by forclosure, or release,
or by any other means whereby, as between individuals, an
equity of redemption can by law be barred.   The present

section after again authorizing this to be done, without any limitation as to the value of the property, further expressly authorizes the bank to exercise powers of sale contained in mortgages.

As to advances for building ships.

72. Every bank advancing money in aid of the building of any ship or vessel shall have the same right of acquiring and holding security upon such ship or vessel, while building and when completed, either by way of mortgage, *hypothèque,* hypethecation, privilege, or lien thereon, or purchase or transfer thereof, as individuals have in the Province wherein such ship or vessel is being built, and for that purpose may avail itself of all such rights and means of obtaining and enforcing such security, and shall be subject to all such obligations, limitations and conditions as are, by the law of such Province, conferred or imposed upon individuals making such advances. (R S.C. cap. 120, sec. 52.)

This would appear to enable the bank to take security for future, as well as past, advances when made in aid of the building of any ship or vessel. It is no doubt intended to promote and encourage the ship-building industries of the Dominion

Warehouse receipts may be taken as collateral security.

73. The bank may acquire and hold any warehouse receipt or bill of lading as collateral security for the payment of any debt incurred in its favor in the course of its banking business; and the warehouse receipt or bill of lading so acquired shall vest in the bank, from the date of the acquisition thereof, all the right and title of the previous holder or owner thereof, or of the person from whom such goods, wares and merchandise were received or acquired by the bank, if the warehouse receipt or bill of lading is made directly in favor of the bank, instead of to the previous holder or owner of such goods, wares and merchandise.   (R.S.C. cap. 120, sec. 53, ss. 2.)

This section and the five following ones are generally known as the Warehouse Receipt Clauses of the Bank Act. They were passed, no'doubt, for the purpose of increasing the purchasing power of the capital employed in mercantile business, by enabling merchants and manufacturers to obtain advances on their goods whilst on hand or in transit and awaiting sale.   For a short review of the previous legislation on this subject, see the judgment of Burton, J., in Smith vs. Merchants Bank, 8 Ont., A.R. at page 19 (1883.) Through the instrumentality of warehouse receipts, acquired in the manner prescribed, the bank is, in effect, authorized to make advances or loans on the security of goods, wares and merchandise.

CONSTITUTIONALITY.

The constitutionality of the warehouse receipt clauses has been questioned.   By the B. N. A. Act the Parliament of Canada has exclusive legislative power over Banks and Banking.   It is contended that these clauses have nothing to do with " Banks and Banking," but deal with " Property and Civil Rights,"—one of the subject matters which by the B. N. A. Act are assigned exclusively to the legislative authority of the Provincial Legislatures.   The Supreme Court of Canada has, however, decided in favor of the constitutionality of these clauses, being of opinion that the Dominion Parliament, having power to legislate on the subject matter of Banking, might, in the legitimate exercise of that power, say that banks might take warehouse receipts as collateral secur ity for the repayment of advances made, even though incidentally such legislation might interfere with " Property and Civil Rights in the Provinces." Merchants Bank of Canada vs. Smith, 8 S.C.R. 512 (1884)—See also on this point Dupuy vs. Cushing, L.R. 5 App. Cas. 409 (1880). In the case of Tennant vs. Union Bank, 19 Ont., R. 1. (1892) now under appeal to the Privy Council, the question of con stitutionality was again formally raised in the Court below so that it might be discussed in the argument of the case in the Privy Council.

" WAREHOUSE RECEIPT."

The expression warehouse receipt used in the above clause is defined in sect. 2, ss. (d) as follows :

" (d). The expression " warehouse receipt " means any " receipt given by any person for any goods, wares, or merchan- " dise, in his actual, visible and continued possession, as " bailee thereof, in good faith, and not as of his own property, " and includes receipts given by any person who is the *owner* " *or* keeper of a harbor, cove, pond, wharf, yard, warehouse, " shed, storehouse or other place *for the storage of goods,* " *wares or merchandise,* for 'goods, wares and merchandise " delivered to him as bailee and actually in the place, or in " one or more of the places *owned or* kept by him, whether " such person is engaged in other business or not ;"

The above definition of a warehouse receipt differs, to some extent, from the one in the preceeding act, R.S,C., cap. 120, sec. 2, ss. (b). The words in italics have been added and the words " *also specification of timber* " have been omitted from the end of the clause.

The definition of " warehouse receipt " was first introduced into the Bank Act by 43 Vic. Cap. 22 sec. 7. It is generally supposed that it was framed to meet the difficulties caused by a series of decisions in Ontario, ending in the cases of the Merchants Bank v. Smith, 8 S.C.R. 512 (1884), and Milloy v. Kerr, 8 S.C.R. 474 (1880), deciding that under the section corresponding nearly to section 73 of this

Act, a warehouse receipt to be valid must be given by a person exercising the business of a warehouseman. It is conceived that under the law as it at present stands, A, a dry goods merchant, can deliver a bale of silk into the possession of B, another dry goods merchant, to be deposited and kept in B's store, B can then issue a valid warehouse receipt to A for this bale of silk.   This is the opinion of Boyd C. in re. Montieth, 10 Ont. R. 529 (1886) where the meaning of the expression "warehouse receipt" as used herein is much discussed. At page 540 of his judgment the Chancellor says : " the " present definition discriminates between two classes of " persons who are authorized to issue receipts.

" 1. Any *bona fide* bailee of goods which are in his actual " visible and continued possession may give receipts therefor. " 2. Any person who is the keeper of a warehouse or other " place for goods can in respect of goods being in that ware- " house or place give such receipts......The same sort of proof " is not required in the case of a warehouseman granting such " documents as in the case of a bailee of goods, and the validity " of such receipts does not necessarily depend upon proof that " the warehouseman was actually, visibly, and continuously in " possession of the goods covered thereby."

The meaning of the expression " warehouse receipt " was again under discussion in Tennant v. Union Bank, 19 Ont. App. R. 1 (1892), and the opinion is expressed that a ware-house receipt given by the keeper of a warehouse, &c., must cover goods in some particular warehouse or place kept by such warehouseman.   Maclennan, J., at page 13 says " The " next question is whether this paper was a good warehouse " receipt under the Bank Act so that the bank might take it " as a security under R.S.C. Cap. 120, sec. 53, ss. 2, " (now sec. 73), the logs having been at the time in " transit from the woods where they were cut, to the mill, " and being as described in the document, in Lakes St. " John and Couchiching en route for Bradford's Mill."

" I think that even if the logs were confined by a boom or " booms in those lakes a warehouse receipt could not be given ' upon them. What the Statute R S.C. cap. 120, sec. 2 (b) says

" is in substance this :   The expression ' warehouse receipt '
" means a receipt given by a person for goods in his actual
" possession as bailee . . . . and includes receipts
" from any person who is keeper of a . . . . mill or
" other place in Canada, for goods in the place so kept by
" him.   I am unable to see how Lakes St. John and Couch-
" iching where these logs were at the date of the receipt, can
" be regarded as place: *kept by the signers of the receipt.*"

Tennant's case was decided under the Bank Act R.S. of C.
c. 120. The change in the language of the definition of " warehouse receipt" in the present Act seems stronger in favor of
the view expressed by Mr. Justice Maclennan.

BILL OF LADING.

Section 2 ss. (e) of the Act defines the expression " bill of
lading " as follows :

" (e.) The expression "bill of lading " includes all receipts
" for goods, wares or merchandise, accompanied by an under-
" taking to transport the same from the place where they were
" received to some other place, whether by land or water, or
" partly by land and partly by water, and by any mode of
" carriage whatever ;"

A bill of lading is a memorandum signed by the
master acknowledging the receipt of goods to be
carried as therein mentioned.   It generally has a two-fold
character, containing not only a receipt for the goods, but
also the contract upon which they are to be carried.   By
the English law its use is confined to maritime adventures.
The above definition however extends its meaning to cover
all receipts for goods to be carried by sea or by land.

GOODS, WARES AND MERCHANDISE.

Section 2, ss. (c) defines these words as follows :

"(c) The expression ' goods, wares and merchandise '
" includes, in addition to the things usually understood there-
" by, timber, deals, boards, staves, saw-logs and other lumber,

"petroleum, crude oil, and all agricultural produce and other
"articles of commerce " ;

These words "goods, wares and merchandise" will be
found used only in the above sub-clause, and in Section 64,
and in the sections of the Act relating to warehouse receipts, viz., Sections 73 to 78 ; as so used they would probably include only "goods, wares and merchandise," dealt
with in a mercantile transaction. Under the English Factors
Acts similar words were held not to include stock certificates
in a joint stock company, see Trueman vs. Appleyard, 32
L. J. Ex. 175 ; 1, N. R. 30, (1862).

COLLATERAL SECURITY.

In Early vs. Early L.R., 16, Chy. D., 214 (1878) and in
In re Athill—Athill vs. Athill L.R., 16, Chy., D. 222 (1880)
the word "collateral" was much discussed and its meaning
was held to be "parallel" or "additional" and not
"secondary."

"DEBTS INCURRED."

Section 73 declares that the bank may acquire and hold
any warehouse receipt or bill of lading as collateral security
for the payment of any debts incurred in its favor in the
course of its banking business.   In order to ascertain the
meaning of the words "debts incurred", as used in this
section, reference must be made to section 75, which in effect
declares that the debts must be incurred at the time when
the warehouse receipt or bill of lading is transferred or promised in writing to be transferred to the bank.

THE BANK MAY ACQUIRE AND HOLD ANY WAREHOUSE RECEIPT, &c.

In a case arising under the C.S.C., cap. 54, and 24 Vic., c.
23 (Can.), where a bank took a warehouse receipt from a
warehouse-man *acknowledging* to have received *from the bank*
6,000 bales of wool deposited in the warehouse, subject to
the order of the bank, it was held by the Ontario Courts, that

such warehouse receipt being given directly to the bank was
wholly inoperative, the language of the statutes then in force
contemplating and authorizing transfers of warehouse receipts
to banks by indorsement only.   See Bank of British North
America vs. Clarkson, 19 U. C. C. P., 182 (1868);   Royal
Canadian Bank vs. Miller, 28 U. C. C. P., 593 (1869).
(In appeal) 29 U. C. Q. B., 266 (1870).   This was a very
rigid construction of the statutes, and was, it is believed, a
surprise to the mercantile community.   An opposite view
had, moreover, been arrived at by the Courts in Quebec,
vide Molsons Bank vs. Janes, 9 L. C. Jur., 81 (1864), and
a less rigid construction had been applied to bills of lading
in the very same year in the Ontario Court of Appeal, *vide*
Royal Canadian Bank vs. Carruthers, 29 U.C.Q.B., 283
(1870); consequently, shortly after the pronouncing of the
decision in appeal in Ontario, above cited, the language of
the clauses was changed (*vide* 34 Vic., c. 5, s. 46, *et seq.*),
and subsequently, doubts having been again raised, was again
changed (*vide* 43 Vic., c. 22, s. 7).   It is now believed that
the words used in the present Act are large enough to enable
a bank under this section, to acquire title to a warehouse
receipt, either directly from the warehouseman, or by way of
endorsement from the holder thereof,—See Merchants Bank
of Canada vs. Smith, 8 S.C.R., 512 (1884); 8 Ont. App. R.,
15 (1883); 28 Gr. 629 (1881); and see B. of Hamilton vs.
Noye, 9 Ont. R. at p. 631 (1885).

BY WHOM MAY THE WAREHOUSE RECEIPT BE GIVEN ?

It may undoubtedly be given by the borrower from the
bank.   But may it be given by anybody else?   In Tennant
vs. Union Bank, 19 Ont., App. R. at p. 6 (1892), Mr.
Justice Osler answers this question   "It does not appear to
" be essential that the borrower should be the holder or owner
" of a warehouse receipt. The bank may acquire it as collat-
" eral security for him from a third party."

It is now declared by this section, that the warehouse
receipt or bill of lading, so acquired, shall vest in the bank,
from the date of the acquisition thereof, all the right and

title :—(1) "Of the previous *holder* or *owner* thereof" (thereby implying that there must be a previous holder or owner of of the warehouse receipt or bill of lading) ; or, (2) *"Of the person from whom such goods, wares, or merchandise were re-ceived or acquired by the bank, if the warehouse receipt or bill of lading is made directly in favor of the bank, instead of to the previous holder or owner of such goods, wares or merchandise."* These latter words *in italics* were added by 43 Vic. c. 22, s. 7 (1880), probably in anticipation of an objection which was afterwards raised in the Court of Appeal in Ontario in Merchant's Bank of Canada vs. Smith, (1883), (8 Ont. App. R. 15), that even under the wide language used in 34 Vic., c. 5, s. 46, it is still necessary that there should be *a previous holder or owner* of the warehouse receipt or bill of lading before it can be validly transferred to or acquired by the bank.

Under the present law a warehouse receipt given directly to the bank by the bailee or warehousemen, would certainly be good.

EFFECT OF THE ACQUISITION OF THE WAREHOUSE RECEIPT

The section now declares that the warehouse receipt or bill of lading, acquired under the act, shall vest in the bank from the date of the acquisition thereof, all the right and title :—(1) *"Of the previous holder or owner thereof"* or, (2) *"Of the person from whom such goods, wares or merchandise were received or acquired by the bank, if the warehouse receipt or bill of lading is made directly in favor of the bank, instead of to the previous holder or owner of such goods, wares or merchandise."*

A recent case on the subject is The Dominion Bank v. Davidson, 12 Ont. App. R. 90 (1886), in which the facts were as follows :—The execution debtors, Chapman & Son, bought the oats in question from the owners thereof, who shipped them to Toronto consigned to their own order or to the order of some bank other than the plaintiffs', sending the shipping receipt, with a draft for the price of the oats attached, to Chapman & Son at Toronto. The latter then took the shipping receipt to the plaintiff bank who advanced the money thereon to pay the draft, returning the shipping receipt to Chapman & Son for the purpose of getting same endorsed by consignee thereof and obtaining the oats from the carriers, first taking from Chapman & Son a receipt in these words :—

"Received in trust from the Dominion Bank bill of lading for   bushels oats, and I hereby undertake to sell the property specified for said bank and collect the proceeds of sale or sales thereof and deposit the same with the said bank, in Toronto, to the credit of same, I hereby acknow- ledging myself to be bailee of the said property for the said Bank."

Chapman & Son received the oats from the carriers and warehoused them, taking warehouse receipts in their own name, which they endorsed to the plaintiff bank who gave up the bailee receipt.

Held, that no property in the oats had passed to Chapman & Son when the plaintiffs made the advance, and that the latter were therefore entitled at least as equitable owners, as against execution creditors of Chapman & Son,—and held also that the Chattel Mortgage Act could have no applica- tion, for when the oats first came into the possession of Chapman & Son, they came charged with or subject to the plaintiffs' title.

Another recent case is Tennant v. Union Bank, 19 Ont. App. R. 1 (1892).

GOODS SHOULD BE DESCRIBED IN RECEIPT WITH REASONABLE
CERTAINTY—ARE SUBSTITUTED GOODS COVERED ?
EFFECT OF CONVERSION OF PROPERTY.

When taking warehouse receipts, the goods intended to be covered thereby should be described therein with reasonable certainty, and the agent of the bank should, if possible, see that the goods themselves are in the warehouse and separated from other goods of a similar class. The receipt only covers the actual goods mentioned therein ; it does not ordinarily cover substituted goods. This was expressly

decided in Llado v. Morgan, 23 U.C.C.P., 525 (1874). In
that case the receipt covered thirty bales of corks, and the
court held that it covered the specific bales, and those only,
in the warehouse at the time of the giving of the same
Where, however, there is a custom or usage of trade, (such
as exists in the grain trade), not to deliver back the specific
goods, but the same quantity of goods of a similar kind and
quality (or such as exists in the milling business, not to
deliver back the wheat at all but its equivalent in flour) the
operation of the receipt would probably not be restricted as
in Llado v. Morgan.

See on this point Wilmot v. Maitland, 3 Gr., 107 (1851), in
which a usage in the flour trade is mentioned.

Coffee v. The Quebec Bank, 20 U.C.C.P., 111 and 555
(1869), in which the nature and consequences of the usage
in the grain trade are discussed.

Mason v. Great Western Ry. Co., 31 U.C.Q.B., 73 (1874)
in which the nature and consequences of the usage in the
milling trade are discussed.

Where the warehouseman improperly mixes the goods
covered by the warehouse receipt, with his own goods, especially where in the warehouse receipt he promises to keep the
goods separate; the holder of the receipt, as against the warehouseman himself and as against his assignee in insolvency
or for the benefit of creditors, is entitled to be satisfied out
of similar goods in the warehouse, to the quantity mentioned
in the warehouse receipt. Merchants Bank of Canada v.
Smith, 28, Gr., pp. 638-639 (1881). Great Western Ry,
Co. v. Hodgson, 44 U.C.Q.B., 196 (1879). Bank of Hamilton v. Noye, 9 Ont. R, 631 (1885). Re Goodfallow,
Traders Bank v. Goodfallow, 19 Ont. Rep. 299 (1890).
See also in re Coleman, 36 U.C.Q B., 564 (1875).

REMEDIES OF THE BANK AFTER REFUSAL TO DELIVER.

After demand of delivery and refusal to deliver, the bank,
if possession of the goods covered by the warehouse receipt
can be obtained without force, can take possession of the
same, even though on the land of the warehouseman, with-

out being liable in trespass.   Traders Bank v. Brown Manufacturing Company, 18 Ont. Rep. 430 (1889).

It has been decided that on the re-endorsement of a warehouse receipt by the bank, the pledgor is in as of his original title, and that his rights must be considered as if the bank had never intervened.   Mason v. The Great Western Ry. Co., 31 U.C.Q.B., 73 (1871).   ·

There is an Act in force in Ontario relating to warehouse receipts, viz. R.S. of Ont. (1887) cap. 122, sections 14 et seq.

2. If the previous holder of such warehouse receipt or bill of lading is the agent of the owner of the goods, wares and merchandise mentioned therein, the bank shall be vested with all the right and title of the owner thereof, subject to his right to have the same re-transferred to him, if the debt, as security for which they are held by the bank, is paid : (R.S.C. cap. 120, sec. 53, s.s. 3.)

When previous holder is an agent.

It will be noticed that the language used in this sub-section still is "*if the previous holder* of such warehouse receipt" is the agent, &c., consequently it may be held that "an agent" must *transfer an existing warehouse receipt* to the bank. See on this point notes to section 73 and the remarks of the Ontario Court of Appeal in Merchants Bank of Canada vs. Smith, 8 Ont. App. R. 15 (1883).

· This sub-section enables an agent, in certain cases, to create in favor of a bank, a valid pledge on goods belonging to his principal, even though such pledge may be a wrongful and unlawful dealing with the goods as between the agent and the principal.

MEANING OF THE WORD "AGENT".

The definition of "agent", as used in section 73, will be

found in sec. 73, ss. 3, and is as follows: "The expression
" 'agent' means any person intrusted with the possession of
"goods, wares and merchandise, or to whom the same are
" consigned, or who is possessed of any bill of lading, receipt,
": order, or other document used in the course of business as
" proof of the possession or control of goods, wares and
" merchandise, or authorizing or purporting to authorize,
" either by indorsement or by delivery, the possessor of such
" document to transfer or receive the goods, wares and me:-
" chandise thereby represented ; and such person shall be
" deemed the possessor of such goods, wares and merchan-
" dise, bill of lading, receipt, order, or other document as
" aforesaid, as well if the same are held by any person for
" him or subject to his control as if he is in actual possession
" thereof."

It is no doubt founded on the definition of Agent given
in the Consolidated Statutes of Canada, chapter 59, which is
itself based on the English Factors Acts 4 Geo. IV. cap. 83 ;
6 Geo. IV. cap. 94 ; and 5 and 6 Vic. cap. 39 ; see also R.S.
of Ontario (1887) cap. 128.   The present definition of
Agent is not, however, identical with its definition in the
above Statutes.   In some respects the present definition is
much wider, especially in regard to the possession of documents of title.   In the Consolidated Statutes, chapter 59,
the agent must be "entrusted with " the possession of goods,
or "entrusted with " the possession of the documents of
the title thereto.   By section 73, ss. 3, of this Act it is declared that " Agent " shall mean "any person entrusted with
the possession of goods . . . . or who is possessed
(not "entrusted with " the possession) of any document of
title.   When this question—Who is an agent within the
meaning of this sub-section and section 73, ss. 3—comes up
before the Courts, for decision, we think it will be answered,
that only those persons who are agents within the meaning of
the English Factors Acts and the Consolidated Statutes of
Canada, chapter 59 and R.S. of Ontario, cap. 128, are agents
under this Act.   It may, consequently, be useful to state the

views which have been adopt~d in England on this question
of

WHO IS AN AGENT UNDER THE FACTORS ACTS ?

Now it has been held in Heyman v. Flewker, 13 C. B. N. S.
519 (1863), that the term "agent," under the Factors Acts,
does not include a mere servant or caretaker, or one who
has possession of goods for carriage, safe custody or otherwise, as an independent contracting party, but only *"persons,
whose employment corresponds to that of some known kind of
commercial agent like that class (Factors) from which the Act
has taken its name."* In Cole v. North Western Bank, L.R.
10 C. P. 369 (1875), which contains a most elaborate review
of the Factors Acts and the decisions thereon, Mr. Justice
Blackburn says : "If a furnished house be let to one who
carries on the business of an auctioneer, he is entrusted as
tenant with the furniture, being in tact an auctioneer ; but it
never was the common law, and could not be intended to be
enacted, that, if he carried the furniture to his auction room
and there sold it, he could confer any better title on the purchaser than if he had as auctioneer acted for some other
tenant who committed a similar larceny, as a fraudulent bailee:
nor, to come nearer to the present case, that a warehouseman
or wharfinger, who, as such, is intrusted with the custody of
goods, if he happens also to pursue the trade of a factor, can
give a better title by the sale of the goods than if they had
been intrusted to some other warehouseman who employed
him to sell." See also Johnson v. Credit Lyonnais, L. R.
3 C. P. D, 32 (1877).

In the City Bank v. Barrow, L. R. 5 App Cas. 664 (1880),
a tanner in Montreal received from a merchant in England
hides to be tanned and it was agreed that freight was to be
procured for them by the tanner and the hides returned to
England ; they were tanned, and freight was accordingly
procured for them, but in the meantime the tanner had obtained from the Toronto Bank advances on his own account
on bills, and hypothecated the hides to the bankers as security for such advances, engaging to hand over to them the
bills of lading if his bills of exchange were not duly honored.

They were not duly honored, and the bankers (who had acted in entire ignorance of the transaction between the merchant and the tanner) claimed to retain the bills of lading and the hides until their demands were satisfied. The House of Lords, however, decided that the tanner was not a factor or agent entitled to pledge under any law, Canadian or English, and that the Bank of Toronto acquired no valid lien on the hides, either under the Civil Code, the Consolidated Statutes of Canada, Cap. 59, or the Bank Act.

Lord Selborne, in the course of his judgment, at page 673, says : " It is manifest that the operation of these Factors clauses under the Canadian Code (which is the same as Consolidated Statutes of Canada, c. 59, in this respect) is the same as the operation of the Factors Acts in England in a similar case.   They are taken almost entirely from the English Factors Acts."   Again, at page 675, he says : " I do not propose to dwell longer upon the case.   The Bankers Act seems to me to carry it no further.   It is true it refers to the Consolidated Statutes and not to the Code ; but the code is on this point, only a repetition of the Consolidated Statutes, and is a legislative declaration of the true meaning of those former statutes which are incorporated in it."

Lord Blackburn, in the course of his judgment, at page 678, says : " It is sufficient to say, briefly, that the decision in Cole v. the North-Western Bank (from which an extract is given above) comes to this : that an agent who can pledge or sell must be an agent of that class which, like factors, (taking almost the words of Mr. Justice Willis in the case which has already been referred to of Heyman v. Flewker) have a business which, when carried to its legitimate result, would properly end in selling or in receiving payment for goods.   That would be a kind of class ; factors, and agents in the class of factors.   If such a person is " entrusted " and " *is entrusted in that capacity*," then, in the absence of bad faith on the part of the pledgee, the pledge is good."

See also Bush v. Fry, 15 Ont. R. p. 122 (1887), where the meaning of the word agent under the R S. of Ont. (1887) Cap. 128, was discussed.   See also the remarks of Burton J.

in Tennant v. Union Bank, 19 Ont. R. at pp. 28 and 29 (1892).

The meaning of the words "and such person shall be deemed the possessor of goods or documents of title as well if the same are held by any person for him or sub- ject to his control as if he is in actual possession thereof," as used in the concluding part of the definition of agent in sec- tion 73, ss. 3, will be found discussed in the case of Portalis v. Tetley, L.R. 5 Eq. 140 (1867) where it was held that "a factor by pledging goods in his possession or under his con- trol, as agent, for an amount which did not exhaust their value had not thereby parted with his control over the goods, so as to preclude himself from making a further pledge for the balance of their value, which should be valid as against the principal under the Factors Acts."

AS TO NOTICE OR KNOWLEDGE OF AGENCY.

Under this Act no provisions are made similar to those in the Factors Acts as to the effect of notice to the bank of the fact of the person pledging being an agent.

It is submitted that the bank's title to a warehouse receipt

(1) would be invalid if the bank had notice that the agent pledging had no power to pledge ;

(2) Would be valid if the bank had notice that the agent pledging was an agent but had no notice that such agent was exceeding his powers as between him and his principal ;

(3) Would be valid à fortiori if the bank had no notice that the person pledging was an agent.

Interpretation of "Agent."

3. In this section the expression "agent" means any person intrusted with the possession of goods, wares and merchandise, or to whom the same are consigned, or who is possessed of any bill of lading, receipt, order, or other docu- ment used in the course of business as proof of the possession or control of goods, wares and

merchandise, or authorizing or purporting to authorize, either by indorsement or by delivery, the possessor of such document to transfer or receive the goods, wares and merchandise there · by represented ; and such person shall be deemed the possessor of such goods, wares and merchandise, bill of lading, receipt, order, or other document as aforesaid, as well if the same are held by any person for him or subject to his control as if he is in actual possession thereof. (R.S.C., cap. 120, sec. 53.)

See notes to preceding sub-section.

74. The bank may lend money to any person engaged in business as a wholesale manufacturer of any goods, wares and merchandise, upon the security of the goods, wares and merchandise manufactured by him or procured for such manufacture : *Loans to wholesale manufacturers*

2. The bank may also lend money to any wholesale purchaser or shipper of products of agriculture, the forest and mine, or the sea, lakes and rivers, or to any wholesale purchaser or shipper of live stock or dead stock, and the products thereof, upon the security of such products, or of such live stock or dead stock, and the products thereof : *Loans to certain wholesale purchasers or shippers.*

3. Such security may be given by the owner and may be taken in the form set forth in Schedule C to this act, or to the like effect ; and by virtue of such security, the bank shall acquire *Form of security.*

the same rights and powers in respect to the goods, wares and merchandise, stock or products covered thereby, as if it had acquired the same by virtue of a warehouse receipt. (New. Substituted for R.S.C., cap. 120, sec. 54.)

MANUFACTURER.

The word ' Manufacturer ' is by sec. 2, ss. (f,) defined as follows : " The word " manufacturer " includes malsters, dis-" tillers, brewers, refiners and producers of petroleum, tanners, " curers, packers, canners of meat, pork, fish, fruit or veget-" ables, and any person who produces by hand, art, process " or mechanical means any goods, wares or merchandise."

GOODS, WARES AND MERCHANDISE.

This expression is by sec. 2, ss. (c,) defined as follows : " The expression ' goods, wares and merchandise ' includes " in addition to the things usually understood thereby, timber, " deals, boards, staves, sawlogs and other lumber, petroleum, " crude oil, and all agricultural produce and other articles of " commerce ; "

The previous Bank Acts contained a section, which has been omitted from this act, giving power to persons exercising certain trades to issue warehouse receipts by way of security to a bank on their own goods, wares and merchanise stored in their own yards or warehouses.—(See R.S.C., cap. 120, sec. 54.)

In lieu of this omitted section, the present section has been substituted. It empowers a bank to lend money to wholesale manufacturers (as above defined) upon the security of goods, wares and merchandise manufactured by them or procured for such manufacture. It further empowers a bank to lend money to any wholesale purchaser or wholesale shipper of certain products, and live and dead stock as mentioned in sub-section 2, of the above section upon the security of such products and live and dead stock.

SECURITY—BY WHOM TO BE GIVEN.

Sub-section 3 provides that the security hereunder may be given by the owner—it seems to us that in most, if not in all cases, the security must be given by him. It seems questionable if it can be given by an agent. Section 73 seems to imit the power of agents to the giving of warehouse receipts as thereby provided for. No pledge of goods to the bank is valid unless authorized by the act, (see sec. 64). No express authority is given, by this or any other section, to agents to pledge under section 74, and we can find no implied authority unless it is conferred by that part of sub-section 3, which declares that the bank shall acquire the same rights to the goods covered by the security as if it had acquired the same by virtue of a warehouse receipt.

SECURITY, IN WHAT FORM.

The security may be taken in the form set forth in Schedule C. to this Act, or to the like effect.

The form given in Schedule C. is as follows :—

In consideration of an advance of   dollars, made by the (*name of bank*) to A.B., for which the said bank holds the following bills or notes (*describe fully the bills or notes held, if any*), the goods, wares and merchandise mentioned below are hereby assigned to the said bank as security for the payment, on or before the   day of of the said advance, together with interest thereon at the rate of   per cent. per annum from the day of   (*or, of the said bills and notes, or renewals thereof, or substitutions therefor, and interest thereon, or as the case may be*).

This security is given under the provisions of section seventy-four of "The Bank Act," and is subject to all the provisions of the said Act.

The said goods, wares and merchandise are now owned by   and are now in   possession, and are free from any mortgage, lien or charge thereon, (*or as the case may be*), and are in (*place or places where goods are*), and are the following : (*particular description of goods assigned*).

Dated at   18

FOR WHAT INDEBTEDNESS CAN THE SECURITY BE TAKEN ?

The section itself provides that the bank may lend the money upon the security. The form, Schedule C, by the use of the word "advances," indicates that the bank may advance the money upon the security—the 75th section, however, finally determines the powers of the bank in this respect. The security must be given or must be promised in writing to be given to the bank cotemporaneously with the advance.

EFFECT OF THE SECURITY WHEN GIVEN, AND POWERS, RIGHTS, AND REMEDIES OF THE BANK THEREUNDER.

This is declared in sub-section 3 :—The bank shall possess the same rights and powers, under the security over the goods covered thereby as it would possess under a warehouse receipt, covering such goods, duly acquired under the other sections of the Act.   See sections 73, 75, 76, 77 and 78.

A doubt has been raised whether the security created under sec. 74 would be valid in Ontario without registration, as required by the Chattel Mortgage Act. We think that no registration of the security is requisite to perserve its validity. We think that the rights of the bank to demand and take possession of the goods covered by the security are the same as if it held a warehouse receipt covering such goods. See on this point notes to section 73.

If the debtor, after the maturity of the debt, wilfully withholds from the bank possession of the goods upon demand, he is liable to be punished criminally.   See sec. 75, ss. 4.

GENERAL REMARKS.

This section has not yet been the subject of judicial decision, the general tendency of the courts, however, especially in Ontario, has been to restrict rather than enlarge the lan-

guage of the warehouse clauses of the Bank Act.   Some of
the judges seem to entertain strong views against the policy
of these clauses and their decisions reflect their views.   The
probability is that this section will receive a pretty strict and
rigid construction when it is presented to the Courts for interpretation.   In view, therefore, of this tendency it would be
wise in drawing a security hereunder to give as full a description of the goods and of their locality as the nature of the
case admits of.   In Tennant's case, 19 App. R. 1 (1892)
referred   to   in   the   notes   to   section   73,   it   was
intimated   that   logs   lying   in   rivers   and   in   transit
from the timber limits where they were cut, to the mills
where they were to be sawn, could not be pledged under the
then Bank Act, because they could not be said to be in a place
or places kept by the person pledging the same.   We think
that logs so situated can be pledged under this section.

75. The bank shall not acquire or hold any *When such*
warehouse receipt or bill of lading or security *security may
be acquired.*
under the next preceding section to secure the
payment of any bill, note or debt, unless such
bill, note or debt is negotiated or contracted at
the time of the acquisition thereof by the bank,
or upon the written promise or agreement that
such warehouse receipt or bill of lading or security would be given to the bank; but such
bill, note or debt may be renewed, or the time
for the payment thereof extended, without
affecting any such security: (R.S.C. cap. 120,
sec. 53, ss. 4, changed.)

To negotiate is to transfer for valuable consideration, per
Richards J, in Foster vs. Bowes, 2 Ont. P.R. 256 (1857).
Where a bank holds warehouse receipts to collaterally secure
the payment of notes, and the notes become overdue, and an
extension of time is agreed on, the delivery up of the receipts

and overdue notes, being a surrender of the bank's lien, is a valuable consideration for and therefore a negotiation of the new renewal notes, or else it is only a substitution or continuation of the securities.   Bank of Hamilton vs. Noye, 9 O. R. 637 (1885).

But when there is a simple renewal of existing paper and the taking of warehouse receipts on such renewal—no new advance being made and no valuable consideration given or surrendered contemporaneously by the bank which might represent the inception of a new transaction or negotiation of securities, Boyd, Chancellor, held the warehouse receipts invalid—Dominion Bank vs. Oliver, 17 Ont. R. 402 (1889).

In some of the former statutes the word " understanding ' was used.   It was afterwards changed to the word "promise." This act makes a further change and requires that there must be a " written promise or agreement."

This section prohibits the bank from acquiring a warehouse receipt or bill of lading or security under section 74 to secure the payment of any bill, note or debt unless,

(1) Such bill or note is negotiated or debt contracted at the time of the acquisition of such warehouse receipt or bill of lading or security by the bank.

(2) Or unless such bill or note is negotiated or debt contracted upon the written promise or agreement that such warehouse receipt or bill of lading or security will afterwards be given or transferred to the bank.

Consequently, in The Royal Canadian Bank vs. Ross, 40 U.C.Q.B., 466 (1877), it was held,

FIRSTLY ;—that the corresponding sections in 34 Vic. c. 5, secs. 46 and 47, permit the transfer to a bank of a bill o lading or warehouse receipt to secure an antecedent debt where the "promise " at the time of contracting such debt was that the bill of lading or warehouse receipt should thereafter be transferred as collateral security therefor :

SECONDLY ;—that an agreement made at the time the debt was incurred to the bank, to give warehouse receipts on goods which the person at the time of the making of the agreement is not possessed of, if followed by the subsequent giving of such warehouse receipt, in pursuance of such agreement, gives to the bank a valid charge thereon under this section (see specially p.p. 467, 475 and 476).   About the same time a similar decision was reached by the Court of Chancery in Ontario, reported as Suter vs. The Merchants Bank of Canada, 24 Gr. 374, (1877).

See also McCrae vs. Molson's Bank, 25 Gr. 519, (1878).

Bank of Hamilton vs. Noye, 9 Ont. R. 630 (1885).

Cockburn vs. Sylvester, 1 Ont. A. R. 471 (1877), over-ruling in re Coleman, 36, U.C.Q. B. 564, (1875).

It was held in the case of Cockburn vs. Sylvester, just re-ferred to, that there is no "debt" contracted, within the meaning of this section, by a drawer to an accommodation acceptor, at the time of the giving of such accommodation acceptance so as to support a concurrent endorsement, by such drawer to such accommodation acceptor, of a ware-house receipt, although it is quite possible that a debt may arise by reason of the acceptor being subsequently com-pelled to pay the acceptance.

As to the meaning of the words "debts contracted" see notes to section 68.

If the warehouse receipt, bill of lading or security is validly acquired, the debt or bill or note representing same, may be renewed, from time to time, without affecting the security.

2. **The bank may, on shipment of any goods, wares and merchandise for which it holds a warehouse receipt, or security as aforesaid, surrender such receipt or security and receive a bill of lading in exchange therefor, or, on the receipt of any goods, wares and merchandise for which it holds a bill of lading or security, as aforesaid, it may surrender such bill of lading or security, store such goods, wares and merchan-dise, and take a warehouse receipt therefor, or**

Exchange of warehouse re-ceipt for bill of lading and vice versa.

may ship them, or part of them, and take
another bill of lading therefor :

This subsection was first added to the Bank Act in 1880.
It declares that the goods covered by the warehouse receipt
or security under Sec. 74, may be transported from one
place to another without destroying the lien of the bank
thereon. It thus facilitates the marketing of the goods.

It would seem to us that without the aid of this section
the bank, so soon as it had acquired a valid title to a warehouse receipt under the act, could demand delivery of the
goods according to the tenor of the warehouseman's undertaking and having acquired possession of the goods, could
ship them or store them as it pleased. It will be observed
that the powers expressly given by this section, are extended
to goods assigned to the bank as security under the new
section 74 as well as to goods secured by warehouse receipts.

Penalty for
making false
statement.

3. Everyone is guilty of a misdemeanor and
liable to imprisonment for a term not exceeding
two years, who wilfully makes any false statement in any warehouse receipt, bill of lading or
security, as aforesaid. (R.S.C. cap. 120, sec. 53,
ss. 7.)

Penalty for
alienating
goods so secur-
ed.

4. Every one is guilty of a misdemeanor and
liable to imprisonment for a term not exceeding
two years, who, having possession or control of
any goods, wares and merchandise covered by
any warehouse receipt, bill of lading or security as aforesaid, and having knowledge of such
receipt, bill of lading or security, and without
consent of the bank, in writing and before the
advance, bill, note or debt thereby secured has
been fully paid, wilfully alienates or parts with
any such goods, wares, or merchandise, or wil-

fully withholds from the bank possession thereof upon demand after default in payment of
such advance, bill, note or debt. (New.)

See further as to criminal offences in connection with
warehouse receipts and as to the punishment therefor, sections 376, 377 and 378 of the Criminal Code of 1892,
which comes into force on the first day of July 1893.

The above sections will be found herein printed after the
Bank Act.

76. If goods, wares and merchandise are
manufactured or produced from the goods, wares
and merchandise, or any of them, included in or
covered by any warehouse receipt, or security
given under section seventy-four of this Act,
while so covered, the bank holding such warehouse receipt or security shall hold or continue to
hold such goods, wares and merchandise, during
the process and after the completion of such
manufacture or production, with the same right
and title and for the same purposes and upon
the same conditions as it held or could have
held the original goods, wares and merchandise. (R.S.C. cap. 120, sec. 56, changed so as
to bring all classes of goods within its operation)

As to goods manufactured from articles pledged.

It was said in the case of Mason vs. Great Western Ry.
Co., 31 U.C.Q.B. 73 (1871), that where wheat is delivered
to a miller and an equivalent quantity of flour delivered in
exchange, the flour should be considered the produce of the
wheat by the custom of trade. See also on this same point
Coffee vs. The Quebec Bank, 20 U.C.C.P. 110 (1869) and
555 (1870); In re Coleman 36 U.C.Q.B. 559 (1875); Bank
of Hamilton vs. Noye, 9 Ont. R. 63 (1885).

Prior claim of the bank over unpaid vendor

77. All advances made on the security of any bill of lading or warehouse receipt, or security given under section seventy-four of this Act, shall give to the bank making such advances a claim for the repayment of such advances on the goods, wares and merchandise therein mentioned, or into which they have been converted, prior to and by preference over the claim of any unpaid vendor ; but such preference shall not be given over the claim of any unpaid vendor who had a lien upon such goods, wares and merchandise at the time of the acquisition by the bank of such warehouse receipt, bill of lading, or security, unless the same was acquired without knowledge on the part of the bank of such lien. (R.S.C. cap. 120, sec. 57, slightly changed.)

" OR INTO WHICH THEY HAVE BEEN CONVERTED."

Where goods covered by a warehouse receipt are manufactured or converted into something else, this clause recognises the right of the holder of the warehouse receipt or security under sec. 74 to a lien on such new product :—see also the preceding section.

It would seem to us that the lien holder would have been entitled to follow the products of the goods covered by this warehouse receipt so long as he could have identified them quite apart from any special legislation on the subject.

" AND BY PREFERENCE OVER THE CLAIM OF ANY UNPAID VENDOR."

These words probably have reference to the privilege of the unpaid vendor under sections 1998 to 2000 of the Civil Code of Lower Canada.

78. In the event of the non-payment at ma- Sale of goods on non-pay- ment of debt. turity of any debt secured by a warehouse receipt or bill of lading, or security given under section seventy-four of this Act, the bank may sell the goods, wares and merchandise mentioned therein, or so much thereof as will suffice to pay such debt with interest and expenses, returning the overplus, if any, to the person from whom such warehouse receipt, or bill of lading, or security, or the goods, wares and merchandise mentioned therein, as the case may be, were acquired; but such power of sale shall be subject to the following provisions, namely :—(R.S.C., cap. 120, sec. 55, slightly changed.)

2. No sale without the consent in writing of Notice to be given before sale of goods pledged. the owner of any timber, boards, deals, staves, saw logs or other lumber, shall be made under this Act until notice of the time and place of such sale has been given by a registered letter, mailed in the post office to the last known address of the pledger thereof, at least thirty days prior to the sale thereof; and no goods, wares and merchandise, other than timber, boards, deals, staves, saw logs or other lumber, shall be sold by the bank under this Act without the consent of the owner, until notice of the time and place of sale has been given by a registered letter, mailed in the post office to the last known address of the pledger thereof, at least ten days prior to the sale thereof: (R.S.C., cap. 120, sec. 78, ss. 2.)

Sale by auc-
tion after no-
tice.

3. Every such sale of any article mentioned in this section, without the consent of the owner, shall be made by public auction, after a notice thereof by advertisement, stating the time and place thereof, in at least two newspapers published in or nearest to the place where the sale is to be made; and if such sale is in the Province of Quebec, then at least one of such newspapers shall be a newspaper published in the English language, and one other such newspaper shall be a newspaper published in the French language. (R.S.C., cap. 120, sec. 78, ss. 3.)

Section 78 and its sub-sections confer on a bank, on default in payment of its debt, power to sell the goods, wares and merchandise pledged to it under a bill of lading, a warehouse receipt, or a security taken under section 74 of this Act, but such power of sale is made subject to certain conditions.

IN THE FIRST PLACE.—Without the written consent of the vendor no sale shall be made until the bank has given to the pledger in the manner prescribed, thirty days notice at least in the case of timber, boards, deals, staves, saw logs or other lumber, and ten days notice at least in the case of other goods, wares and merchandise of the time and place of such sale. (See sub-section 2.)

IN THE NEXT PLACE.—The sale must be by public auction and must be advertised as prescribed in sub-section 3.

Suppose the bank disregarded the provisions of sub-sections 2 and 3, would the sale be void, so as to give no title to a *bona fide* purchaser of the goods from the bank, or would the sale be good, and the bank liable to an action at the suit of the pledger of the goods? In other words are the provisions directory or imperative.

Now section 78, sub-section 1, which gives the power to sell, declares that such power shall be subject to the following provisions; and sub-section 2 declares that no sale shall be made unless notice thereof is given as thereby prescribed. It would seem to us, therefore, that the giving of this notice in the manner prescribed is imperative, and that the power to sell only arises after this requirement has been duly fulfilled.

It would follow therefore that unless the notices were given as prescribed by the Act the sale would be invalid.

The requirements of sub-section 3 are couched in affirmative language only. They are requirements regulating the conduct of the sale after the power of sale has arisen and, we are inclined to think, are directory only—consequently, the failure to observe them would not make the sale invalid, so as to enable the owner of the goods to follow them into the hands of a purchaser. The owner however, would not be without a remedy as the bank would be liable to him for any damages caused by the non-observance of the statutory requirements.

79. Every bank which violates any provision contained in any of the sections numbered sixty-four to seventy-eight (both inclusive) shall incur for each violation thereof a penalty not exceeding five hundred dollars. (R.S.C. c. 12), sec. 45, ss. 2.) *Penalty for contravention.*

Under the repealed Act penalties were only imposed for breaches of some of the sections which correspond to sections 64 to 78 of this Act.

According to the Bank of Toronto vs. Perkins, 8 S.C.R. 603, (1883), discussed in the notes to section 64, the above penalties are cumulative.

80. The bank shall not be liable to incur any penalty or forfeiture for usury, and may stipulate for, take, reserve or exact any rate of interest or discount not exceeding seven per cent. per annum, and may receive and take in *No penalty for usury.* *What interest may be allowed.*

advance any such rate, but no higher rate of interest shall be recoverable by the bank ; and the bank may allow any rate of interest whatever upon money deposited with it. (R.S.C. cap. 120, sec. 61.)

The general effect of this and the succeeding section is to except contracts of a bank from the operation of the laws relating to usury that may be in force in any of the provinces so that the bank is thereby not only relieved from the pecuniary penalty (if any) mentioned in such laws but the contract and security given for the moneys loaned is saved from forfeiture thereunder. Commercial Bank vs. Cotton, 17, U.C.C.P. 214 and 447, (1867). It would appear that a bank on making a loan may stipulate for any rate of interest or discount without invalidating the contract—but if compelled to sue can only recover from the borrower interest at a rate agreed upon not being more than 7 per cent. per annum, and the collection and agency fees, if any, allowed by sections 82 and 83 ; but in the absence of any agreement for the payment of such interest, the bank if compelled to sue can only recover the interest allowed by the general law on the debt sued on. Royal Canadian Bank vs. Shaw, 21 U.C.C.P. 455, (1871), also C.S.C. cap. 127 sec. 2.

It would appear also that if a bank is actually paid interest in excess of seven per cent. such excess cannot be recovered back by the person who paid the same. See Quinlan vs. Gordon 20 Gr. App. 1, (1861), and Hutton vs. Federal Bank, 9 Ont. Pr. R. 568 (1883).

No instrument to be void on ground of usury.   **81.** No promissory note, bill of exchange or other negotiable security, discounted by or indorsed or otherwise assigned to the bank, shall be held to be void, usurious or tainted by usury, as regards such bank, or any maker, drawer, acceptor, indorser, or indorsee thereof, or other party thereto, or *bona fide* holder thereof, nor shall any party thereto be subject to any penalty or forfeiture by reason of any rate of interest taken, stipulated or received by such bank, on or with respect to such promissory note, bill of exchange, or other negotiable security; or paid or allowed by any party thereto to another in compensation for, or in consideration of the rate of interest taken or to be taken thereon by such bank ; but no party thereto, other than the bank, shall be entitled to recover or liable to pay more than the lawful rate of interest in the Province where the suit is brought, nor shall the bank be entitled to recover a higher rate than seven per cent. per annum ; and no innocent holder of or party to **As to innocent holders.** any promissory note, bill of exchange or other negotiable security, shall, in any case, be deprived of any remedy against any party thereto, or liable to any penalty or forfeiture, by reason of any usury or offence against the laws of any such Province, respecting interest, committed in respect of such note, bill or negotiable security, without the complicity or consent of such innocent holder or party. (R.S.C. cap. 120 sec. 62.)

See notes to preceding section.

82. The bank may, in discounting at any of **Collection fees.** its places of business, branches, agencies or offices of discount and deposit, any note, bill or other negotiable security or paper payable at any other of its own places or seats of business, branches, agencies or offices of discount and deposit in Canada, receive or retain, in addition to the discount, any amount not exceeding the following rates per cent. according to the time it has to run, on the amount of such note, bill or other negotiable security or paper, to defray the expenses attending the collection thereof, that is to say : under thirty days, one-eighth of one per cent ; thirty days or over, but under sixty days, one-fourth of one per cent ; sixty days and over, but under ninety days, three-eighths of one per cent ; ninety days and over, one-half of one per cent.   (R.S.C. cap. 120, sec. 63).

This section authorizes a bank when discounting paper at any of its branches to charge a collection fee at the rate prescribed herein in addition to the discount, for collecting such paper when payable at any other of the branches of such bank.

The next section authorizes a bank, when discounting paper, to charge a similar collection or agency fee at the rate prescribed therein for collecting such paper when payable at places other than one of its own branches and other than the place of discount.

Agency fees.   **83.** The bank may, in discounting any note, bill or other negotiable security or paper *bonâ fide* payable at any place in Canada different from that at which it is discounted, and other than one of its own places or seats of business, branches, agencies or offices of discount and deposit in Canada, receive and retain, in addition to the discount thereon, a sum not exceeding

one-half of one per cent on the amount thereof,
to defray the expences of agency and charges in
collecting the same. (R.S.C. cap. 120, sec. 64).

See notes on preceding clause.

84. The bank may receive deposits from any
person whomsoever, whatever his age, status or
condition in life, and whether such person is
qualified by law to enter into ordinary contracts
or not ; and, from time to time, may repay any
or all of the principal thereof, and may pay the
whole or any part of the interest thereon to
such person, without the authority, aid, assist-
ance or intervention of any person or official being required, unless before such repayment the
money so deposited in and repaid by the bank
is lawfully claimed as the property of some
other person, in which case it may be paid to
the depositor with the consent of the claimant,
or to the claimant with the consent of the depositor : Provided always, that if the person
making any such deposit could not, under the
law of the Province where the deposit is made,
deposit and withdraw money in and from a
bank without this section, the total amount to
be received from such person on deposit shall
not, at any time, exceed the sum of five hundred dollars. (R S.C. cap. 120, sec. 65).

Deposits may be received from persons unable to contract.

Proviso: amount limited.

See also ss. 45, 58, 60 and Schedule D., ss 5 ; and see
also the Bills of Exchange Act, sec. 8, ss. 4.

In *re* Central Bank—Morton and Blocks claims 17 Ont.
R. 574 (1889), Boyd, Chancellor (overruling the master) held
that under the Bank Act, a bank had power to issue deposit

receipts in the following form :—" Received from
"   the sum of $
" which this bank will repay to the said
" or order, with interest at 4 per cent. per annum on receiv-
" ing 15 days' notice. No interest will be allowed unless the
" money remains with this bank six months. This receipt
" to be given up to the bank when payment of either princi-
" pal or interest is required. Signed, for the Central Bank
" of Canada, A. H. Allen, Cashier." He also stated that he
had a very strong opinion that such deposit receipts were
negotiable instruments under which the holders were entitled
to recover as on a promissory note, but that even if they did
not possess all the incidents of promissory notes yet being
meant to be transferred by endorsement, they were so far
negotiable as to pass a good title to a *bona fide* purchaser for
value, taking without notice of any infirmity of title.

It will be observed that the deposit receipts above referred
to were expressed "which this bank will repay to X or order."
Sometimes the expressions used in such receipts are " which
will be accounted for by this bank to X," or "which this
bank will account for to X." It seems to us that when the
question is fairly presented for decision, such receipts expressed in such language will be held to be promissory
notes ; and it may be that though they are made payable to
X simply, and not expressly " to X or order," they may be
still held to be negotiable by virtue of the Bills of Exchange
Act, sec. 8, ss. 4, which is as follows :—" A bill is payable to
" order which is expressed to be so payable or which is ex-
" pressed to be payable to a particular person, and does not
" contain words prohibiting transfer or indicating an inten-
" tion that it should not be transferable ; " so that if it is
desired to make deposit receipts " non-negotiable," it is advisable to change the present wording of them, so as to indicate more clearly the intention that they shall not be transferable. See also Richer v. Voyer L.R. 5 P.C. 461, (1874)
but see also Sibree v. Tripp, 15 M. & W., 23 (1846) and
Hopkins v. Abbott, L.R. 19 Eq. 222 (1875.)

In Saderquist v. Ontario Bank, 14 Ont. R. 586, (1875) 15
A.R. 609, (1889) it was held that when A left his deposit re-

ceipt with B for safe keeping and B forged A's name thereto and got the money from the bank and delivered up the receipt, the bank was still liable to A for the amount of the receipt and interest. The bank may allow any rate of interest on deposits. See sec. 80.

2. The bank shall not be bound to see to the execution of any trust, whether expressed, implied or constructive, to which any deposit made under the authority of this section is subject; and except only in the case of a lawful claim, by some other person before repayment, the receipt of the person in whose name any such deposit stands, or if it stands in the name of two persons the receipt of one, or if in the names of more than two persons the receipt of a majority of such persons, shall be a sufficient discharge to all concerned for the payment of any money payable in respect of such deposit, notwithstanding any trust to which such deposit is then subject, and whether or not the bank sought to be charged with such trust (and with whom the deposit has been made) had notice thereof; and the bank shall not be bound to see to the application of the money paid upon such receipt. (R.S.C. cap. 120 sec. 65 ss. 2.)

Bank not bound to see to trusts in relation to such deposits.

The law relating to trusts to which shares may be subject is contained in sections 43 and 44.

This sub-section deals with the question of trusts to which deposits made under the authority of this section, may be subject and appears to confer very extraordinary powers on joint depositors, enabling as it does one joint depositor to draw out of the bank money deposited to the credit of himself and a co-depositor. In England it has been held that when money is paid into a bank to the joint account of several persons nominatim, it cannot be drawn out by one of them alone, and although generally the rule is that payment of a debt to one of several joint creditors is a good payment to all, it is otherwise under the Law Merchant in cases arising between a banker and his customers making joint deposits with him, Innes vs. Stephenson, 1 M & Rob. 145, (1831) Husband vs. Davis, 10 C.B. 645. (1851) Beyond this the sub-section does not seem to carry the law further than the cases in England have carried it. Thus it has been decided that the relation between a banker and his customer is that of debtor and creditor with the obligation superadded that the banker is bound to repay his debt when called upon so to do by the draft of his customer, Foley vs. Hill, 2 H.L.C. 28, (1848) Goodwin vs. Robarts L.R. 10, Ex. 337, (1875) and money paid into an account in a man's own name is *prima facie* his money and a loan by him to the banker which the banker is bound to repay him. When a man opens an account in his own name with the words " Police account " or " Executor of Jones " superadded thereto, this is notice to the banker that the moneys standing to the credit of that account are moneys on which persons other than the customer may have equitable claims. (*Ex parte* Kingston, L.R. 6 Ch. App. 632 (1871) and Bailey vs. Finch L.R. 7 Q.B. 34.) (1871) Still, notwithstanding this notice, it is the duty of the banker to honor the cheque of the customer drawn on such an account, even though the banker suspects, or even knows that the customer intends to commit a breach of trust, and it is only when the banker makes himself a party to the breach of trust *e. g.* by designedly reaping some benefit from the same, that he renders himself liable to make restitution. Lord Cairns in Grey vs. Johnson L.R. 3 E. & I. App. 1, (1868) thus sums up the law,—" In order to hold a banker justified in refusing to pay a demand of his customer, the customer being an executor, and drawing a cheque as an executor, there must, in the first place, be some misapplication, some breach of trust, intended by the executor, and there must in the second place, as was said by Sir John Leach, in the well known case of Keane vs. Robarts 4 Madd. 357, (1819) be proof that the bankers are privy to the intent to make this misapplication of the trust funds. And to that I think I may safely add, that if it be shewn that any personal benefit to the bankers themselves is designed or stipulated for, that circumstance, above all others, will most readily establish the fact that the bankers are *in privity* with the breach of trust which is about to be committed." And Lord Westbury in the same case says: " Supposing, therefore, that the banker becomes incidentally aware that the customer, being in a fiduciary or a representative capacity, meditates a breach of trust, and draws a cheque for that purpose, the banker, not being interested in the transaction, has no right to refuse payment of the cheque, for if he did so he would be making himself a party to an inquiry as between his customer and a third person. He would be setting up a supposed *jus tertii* as a reason why he should not perform his own distinct obligation to his customer. But then it has been very well settled that if an executor or a trustee who is indebted to a banker, or to another person, having the legal custody of the assets of a trust estate, applies a portion of them in the payment of his own debt to the individual having that custody, the individual receiving the debt has at once not only abundant proof of the breach of trust, but participates in it for his own personal benefit."

See also, Clench vs. Consolidated Bank, 31 U.C.C.P. 169 (1880), and Molson's Bank vs. Corporation of Brockville, 31 U.C.C.P. 174 (1880).

RETURNS BY THE BANK.

85. Monthly returns shall be made by the bank to the Minister of Finance and Receiver General in the form set forth in Schedule D to this Act, and shall be made up and sent in within the first fifteen days of each month, and

Monthly returns to Government.

shall exhibit the condition of the bank on the last juridical day of the month next preceding; and such monthly returns shall be signed by the chief accountant and by the president, or vice president, or the director or principal partner then acting as president, and by the manager, cashier or other principal officer of the bank at its chief place of business: (R.S.C. cap. 120, sec. 66, slightly changed.)

2. Every bank which neglects to make up and send in, as aforesaid, any monthly return required by this section within the time hereby limited, shall incur a penalty of fifty dollars for each and every day after the expiration of such time during which the bank neglects so to make up and send in such return; and the date upon which it appears by the post office stamp or mark upon the envelope or wrapper enclosing such return for transmission to the Minister of Finance and Receiver General, that the same was deposited in the post office, shall be taken *primâ facie*, for the purposes of this section, to be the date upon which such return was made up and sent in. (R.S.C. cap. 120, sec. 66, slightly changed.)

86. The Minister of Finance and Receiver General may also call for special returns from any bank, whenever, in his judgment, they are necessary to afford a full and complete knowledge of its condition : (R.S.C. cap. 120, sec. 67.)

2. Such special returns shall be made and

Penalty for not making up monthly returns in due time.

Special returns may be called for.

signed in the manner and by the persons specified in the next preceding section, and every
bank which neglects to make and send in any
such special return within thirty days from the
date of the demand therefor by the Minister of
Finance and Receiver General shall incur a penalty of five hundred dollars for each and every
day such neglect continues; and the provisions
contained in the last preceding section as to the
prima facie evidence of the date upon which returns are made up and sent in thereunder, shall
apply to returns made under this section : Provided always, that the Minister of Finance and
Receiver General may extend the time for sending in such special returns for such further period, not exceeding thirty days, as he thinks
expedient. (New.)

87. The bank shall, within twenty days after
the close of each calendar year, transmit or deliver to the Minister of Finance and Receiver
General, to be by him laid before Parliament, a
certified list showing the names of the shareholders of the bank on the last day of such calendar year, with their additions and residences,
the number of shares then held by them respectively, and the value at par of such shares :
(R.S.C. cap. 120, sec. 68, slightly changed.)

2. Such list shall be delivered at the Department of Finance, or shall be sent by registered
letter posted at such time that, in the ordinary
course of post, it may be delivered at the said

Department within the time above limited : (R.S.C. cap. 120, sec. 68.)

3. Every bank which neglects to transmit such list in manner aforesaid within the time aforesaid shall incur a penalty of fifty dollars for each and every day during which such neglect continues. (R.S.C cap. 120, sec 68, ss. 2.)

Penalty for neglect to transmit such lists.

88. The bank shall, within twenty days after the close of each calendar year, transmit or deliver to the Minister of Finance and Receiver-General, to be by him laid before Parliament, a return of all dividends which have remained unpaid for more than five years, and also of all amounts or balances in respect to which no transactions have taken place or upon which no interest has been paid during the five years prior to the date of such return : Provided always, that in case of moneys deposited for a fixed period, the period of five years above referred to shall be reckoned from the date of the termination of such fixed period : (New.)

Annual statement of dividends remaining unpaid, &c.

Proviso.

2. Such return shall be signed in the manner required for the monthly returns under section eighty-five of this Act, and shall set forth the name of each shareholder or creditor, his last known address, the amount due, the agency of the bank at which the last transaction took place, and the date thereof; and if such shareholder or creditor is known to the bank to be dead, such return shall show the names and ad-

Details of return

Further details.

dresses of his legal representatives, so far as known to the bank :   (New.)

3. Every bank which neglects to transmit or deliver to the Minister of Finance and Receiver General the return above referred to, within the time hereinbefore limited, shall incur a penalty of fifty dollars for each and every day during which such neglect continues :   (New.)

Penalty for not making annual return.

4. If, in the event of the winding up of the business of the bank in insolvency, or under any general winding-up Act, or otherwise, any moneys payable by the liquidator, either to shareholders or depositors, remain unclaimed for the period of three years from the date of suspension of payment by the bank, or from the commencement of the winding-up of such business, or until the final winding-up of such business if such takes place before the expiration of the said three years, such moneys and all interest thereon shall, notwithstanding any statute of limitations or other Act relating to prescription, be paid to the Minister of Finance and Receiver General, to be held by him subject to all rightful claims on behalf of any person other than the bank ; and in case a claim to any moneys so paid as aforesaid is thereafter established to the satisfaction of the Treasury Board, the Governor in Council shall, on the report of the Treasury Board, direct payment thereof to be made to the person entitled thereto, together with interest on the principal sum there-

Disposal of unclaimed moneys.

of at the rate of three per cent per annum for a period not exceeding six years from the date of payment thereof to the said Minister of Finance and Receiver General as aforesaid : Provided

Proviso. however, that no such interest shall be paid or payable on such principal sum, unless interest thereon was payable by the bank paying the same to the said Minister of Finance and Receiver General : Provided also, that on pay-

Proviso. ment to the Minister of Finance and Receiver General as herein provided, the bank and its assets shall be held to be discharged from further liability for the amounts so paid. (New.)

Requirements as to outstanding notes in case of insolvency. 5. Upon the winding-up of a bank in insolvency or under any general winding up Act, or otherwise, the assignees, liquidators, directors or other officials in charge of such winding-up, shall, before the final distribution of the assets, or within three years from the commencement of the suspension of payment by the bank, whichever shall first happen, pay over to the Minister of Finance and Receiver General a sum out of the assets of the bank equal to the amount then outstanding of the notes intended for circulation issued by the bank; and, upon such payment being made, the bank and its assets shall be relieved from all further liability in respect of such outstanding notes. The sum so paid shall be held by the Minister of Finance and Receiver General and applied for the purpose of redeeming, whenever presented, such outstanding notes, without interest. (New.)

This section is entirely new. It provides for giving notice to the public, through the Parliamentary Blue Books, of unclaimed dividends and unclaimed deposits lying in banks. It also provides, in the case of a winding-up of a bank, for the disposition of the unclaimed moneys held by it and for the redemption of its outstanding circulation.

INSOLVENCY.

89. In the event of the property and assets of the bank being insufficient to pay its debts and liabilities, each shareholder of the bank shall be liable for the deficiency to an amount equal to the par value of the shares held by him, in addition to any amount not paid up on such shares. (R.S.C. cap. 120, sec. 70, slightly changed in language.)

Liability of shareholders in case of insufficiency of assets.

This is known as the double liability clause and renders every shareholder in a bank liable, not only for the amount unpaid upon his shares, but also for a further amount equal to the nominal value of his shares. To ascertain who are the shareholders thus liable see secs. 30 and 96.

As to the effect of irregularities in the acquisition of shares see notes to section 35.

A bill will lie in equity to enforce the double liability of the shareholders of an insolvent bank. But such bill must be on behalf of all the creditors. Brook vs. Bank of Upper Canada, 6 Chy. 249 (1869); 17 Chy. 301 (1870).

It was decided in Lower Canada that a savings bank, holding bank shares as pledgee, is not the owner thereof within the meaning of this section, and therefore not subject to the double liability. A bank whose shares are transferred to a savings bank is presumed to know that they are held by the latter as collateral security, inasmuch as under 34 V., c. 7, s.

18, a savings bank cannot acquire bank shares or hold them except as pledgee. The Exchange Bank of Canada vs. The Montreal City and District Savings Bank, 2 Mont. Rep. 5 (1885).

See also in re Central Bank, Home and Savings Co. Case 18 Ont. App. R. 491 (1891) (where the Home & Savings Co. having advanced money on the security of shares of the Central Bank, which were transferred to and accepted by it in the ordinary absolute form, were held liable as contributories) and notes to section 35.

As to the priorities given by this act on the assets of the bank see section 53.

AS TO SET-OFF BY CONTRIBUTORIES.

A contributory of an insolvent company, who is also a creditor, cannot set off the debt due him by the company against calls made in the course of winding-up proceedings in respect of the double liability imposed by the Bank Act. The obvious reasons for such a conclusion being, as stated by Strong, J. in the Maritime Bank vs. Troop, 16 S.C.R. 456 (1889), at page 458, of his judgment, "that the fund " thus constituted being formed expressly to pay debts and " liabilities, it would be in law a fund which the directors " would hold in trust for the creditors of the bank, and there- " fore that mutuality between the cross demands, which is " an essential requisite in all cases of set-off, would be want- " ing. The money which the shareholder would be called " on to pay would, in this case, be payable into the hands of " the bank or its directors, but it would be so paid to them " as trustees for distribution amongst persons who were " under no cross liability whatever to the shareholders, " namely, the body of creditors of the insolvent bank. . . " As I have already shown the debt due by the shareholders " in respect of a call under the double liability clause is, in " equity and in substance, a debt due, not to the bank, but " to the creditors of the bank—whilst the debt which the " shareholder seeks to set-off is a debt due, not from the " creditors of the bank—but from the banking corporation

" itself ; consequently they are not in any sense " mutual
" debts " ".

The court in the above case held that there is nothing in
the Winding-up Act, R.S.C., cap. 129, which derogates from
the principle requiring mutuality between the cross demands
in order that they may be the subject of set-off.   As to set-
off generally in winding up proceedings see the Winding-up
Act, R.S.C., cap. 129, sec. 57.

90. As a condition of the rights and privi-   Provision as to
leges conferred by this Act or by any Act in   and statute of
amendment thereof, the following provision   limitations.
shall have effect :—The liability of the bank
under any law, custom, or agreement to repay
moneys deposited with it and interest (if any)
and to pay dividends declared and payable on
its capital stock, shall continue notwithstanding
any statute of limitations or any enactment or
law relating to prescription :

2. This section applies to moneys heretofore   Retroaction.
or hereafter deposited, and to dividends heretofore or hereafter declared.   (New).

During the course of the passing of this Act, and the discussion that took place as to the policy of compelling the
banks to publish, periodically, a list of unclaimed dividends,
and of unclaimed balances (see section 88), it became
generally known that by the laws of most of the Provinces,
after the expiration of a certain prescribed period, a bank
could set up the statutes of limitation in answer to a demand
for payment of a dividend by a shareholder, or of a deposit
balance by a customer.   This state of the law was thought
to be unfair to the public and the above section was inserted
in the Act whereby in effect the banks deprive themselves of
the right to avail themselves of the law of limitation in such
cases.

91. Any suspension by the bank of payment of any of its liabilities as they accrue, in specie or Dominion notes, shall, if it continues for ninety days, consecutively, or at intervals within twelve consecutive months, constitute the bank insolvent and operate a forfeiture of its charter or Act of incorporation, so far as regards all further banking operations; and the charter or Act of incorporation shall remain in force only for the purpose of enabling the directors or other lawful authority to make and enforce the calls mentioned in the next following sections of this Act and to wind up its business. (R.S.C., cap. 120, sec. 71, changed).

92. If any suspension of payment in full in specie or Dominion notes of all or any of the notes or other liabilities of the bank continues for three months after the expiration of the time which, under the preceding section, would constitute the bank insolvent, and if no proceedings are taken under any general or special Act for the winding up of the bank, the directors shall make calls on the shareholders thereof, to the amount they deem necessary to pay all the debts and liabilities of the bank, without waiting for the collection of any debts due to it or the sale of any of its assets or property: (R.S.C., cap. 120, sec. 72, slightly changed).

The time during which the suspension of payment continues, is shortened to three months instead of six months.

2. Such calls shall be made at intervals of thirty days, and upon notice to be given thirty days at least prior to the day on which such call shall be payable, and any number of such calls may be made by one resolution; any such call shall not exceed twenty per cent on each share; and payment of such calls may be enforced in like manner as payment of calls on unpaid stock may be enforced; and the first of such calls may be made within ten days after the expiration of the said three months: _{How such calls shall be made and enforced.}

The words "and any number of such calls may be made by one resolution" were added by the Parliamentary Committee when the revision was going through Parliament. As to necessity for these words, see Robertson v. Banque d'Hochelaga, 4 L. N. 314 (1881) and notes to section 31. A bill will lie in equity at the suit of a creditor to enforce the double liability of the shareholders of an insolvent bank. But such bill must be on behalf of all the creditors. Brooke v. Bank of Upper Canada, 16 Chy. 249 (1869); 17 Chy. 301 (1870).

3. Every director who refuses to make or enforce, or to concur in making or enforcing any call under this section, is guilty of a misdemeanor, and liable to imprisonment for any term not exceeding two years, and shall further be personally responsible for any damages suffered by such default (R S.C. cap. 120, sec. 72, ss. 3.) _{Refusal to make calls under this section a misdemeanor.}

93. In the event of proceedings being taken under any general or special winding-up Act, in consequence of the insolvency of the bank, the said calls shall be made in the manner pre- _{Calls under winding-up Act.}

scribed for the making of such calls in such general or special winding-up Act.

See "The Winding-up Act" R.S.C., cap. 129, secs. 48 and 49, as to making of calls, and sections 42 to 55, thereof inclusive, as to rights and liabilities of contributories. See also R.S.C., chapter 129, sections 97 to 104 inclusive, being the sections of said Act relating to banks only.

94. Any failure on the part of any shareholder liable to any such call to pay the same when due, shall operate a forfeiture by such shareholder of all claim in or to any part of the assets of the bank,—such call and any further call thereafter being nevertheless recoverable from him as if no such forfeiture had been incurred.

Forfeiture for non-payment.

95. Nothing in the six sections next preceeding contained shall be construed to alter or diminish the additional liabilities of the directors as hereinbefore mentioned and declared.

Liability of directors not diminished.

As to the additional liabilities of directors see secs. 48, 52, 97 and 99.

96. Persons who, having been shareholders of the bank, have only transferred their shares, or any of them, to others, or registered the transfer thereof within sixty days before the commencement of the suspension of payment by the bank, and persons whose subscriptions to the stock of the bank have been cancelled in manner hereinbefore provided within the said period of sixty days before the commencement

Liability of shareholders who have transferred their stock.

of the suspension of payment by the bank, shall
be liable to all calls on the shares held or subscribed for by them, as if they held such shares
at the time of such suspension of payment, saving their recourse against those by whom such
shares were then actually held. (R.S.C. cap.
120, sec. 97.)

This section deals with the liability of past shareholders.
(See also sections 30 and 89.)

This section has been changed so as to harmonize with
the changed language of section 30. The only other important change in the section is that which makes shareholders
liable, who have transferred their shares within sixty days
(instead of one calendar month) before the commencement
of the suspension of the bank. If A transfers shares to B,
and B transfers to C, and C transfers to D—all the above
transfers being made within sixty days prior to the suspension—A, B, C and D must all be put on the list of contributories. In re Central Bank—Baine's Case, 16 Ont. R., 293
(1888) ; 16 Ont. App. R. 237 (1889) ; Henderson's Case, 17
Ont. R. 110 (1889).

OFFENCES AND PENALTIES.

97. Everyone is guilty of a misdemeanor
and liable to imprisonment for a term not exceeding two years who, being the president,
vice-president, director, principal partner *en com-*
mandite, manager, cashier or other officer of the
bank, wilfully gives or concurs in giving any
creditor of the bank any fraudulent, undue or
unfair preference over other creditors, by giving

President. &c.,
giving undue
preferen e to
any creditor,
guilty of a
misdemeanor.

security to such creditor or by changing the nature of his claim or otherwise howsoever, and shall further be responsible for all damages sustained by any person in consequence of such preference. (R.S.C. cap. 120, sec. 80.)

The defendant was a director and also a creditor of the Exchange Bank to the extent of about $13,000. After a resolution to suspend payment had been passed, the defendant withdrew $10,000 from the bank, with the concurrence of the president thereof. It was held that he had conspired with the president to and had thereby obtained an undue preference over the other creditors. Regina vs. Buntin, 7 L. N. 228, 395 (1884).

Recovery and disposal of penalties

98. The amount of all penalties imposed upon a bank for any violation of this Act shall be recoverable and enforecable with costs, at the suit of Her Majesty, instituted by the Attorney General of Canada, or the Minister of Finance and Receiver General, and such penalties shall belong to the Crown for the public uses of Canada; but the Governor in Council, on the report of the Treasury Board, may direct that any portion of any penalty be remitted or paid to any person, or applied in any manner deemed best adapted to attain the objects of this Act and to secure the due administration thereof. (New).

Making false statement in returns, &c., a misdemeanor, &c.

99. The making of any wilfully false or deceptive statement in any account, statement, return, report or other document respecting the affairs of the bank is, unless it amounts to a higher offence, a misdemeanor punishable by imprisonment for a term not exceeding five years; and every president, vice-president, director, principal partner *en commandite*, auditor, manager, cashier or other officer of the bank, who prepares, signs, approves or concurs in such statement, return, report or document, or uses the same with intent to deceive or mislead any person, shall be held to have wilfully made such false statement, and shall further be responsible for all damages sustained by any person in consequence thereof. (R.S.C. cap. 120, sec. 81.)

An information under this section may be sworn by a non-shareholder, and even by a citizen, who is a debtor of the bank. See Molleur vs. Loupret, 8 L.N. 305 (1885.)

The instruction to the jury "that wilful intent to make a false return may be inferred by the jury from all the circumstances of the case proved to their satisfaction," was held to be correct in Regina vs. Hincks, 2 L.N. 422, 24 L.C.J., 116 (1879).

As to destroying or falsifying books, &c., by directors and officers of a corporation.—See the Criminal Code, 1892, secs. 364 and 365.

As to stealing by officers of a bank.—See the Criminal Code, 1892, secs. 305 and 319.

As to fraudulent breaches of trust.—See the Criminal Code, 1892, sec. 363.

100. Every person assuming or using the title of " bank," " banking company," " banking house," " banking association," or " banking institution," without being authorized so to do by this Act, or by some other Act in force in that behalf, is guilty of an offence against this Act.   (R.S.C. cap. 120, sec. 82, changed.)

This clause was passed to prevent persons doing business as bankers from carrying on such business so as to lead the public to believe them an incorporated bank.

101. Every person, committing an offence declared to be an offence against this Act, shall be liable to a fine not exceeding one thousand dollars, or to imprisonment for a term not exceeding five years, or to both, in the discretion of the court before which the conviction is had. (New.)

Penalty for offence; against this Act.

See preceding section.

PUBLIC NOTICES.

102. The several public notices by this Act required to be given shall, unless otherwise specified, be given by advertisement in one or more newspapers published at the place where the head office of the bank is situate, and in the *Canada Gazette.* (R.S.C., cap. 120, sec. 84, slightly changed).

How notices shall be given.

DOMINION GOVERNMENT CHEQUES.

103. The bank shall not charge any discount or commission for cashing any official cheque of the Government of Canada, or of any department thereof, whether drawn on itself or on another bank.   (New).

Government cheques to be paid at par.

COMMENCEMENT OF ACT AND REPEAL.

104. This Act shall come into force on the first day of July, in the year one thousand eight hundred and ninety-one ; and from that day chapter one hundred and twenty of the Revised Statutes of Canada, intituled " *An Act Respecting Banks and Banking*," the Act passed in the fifty-first year of Her Majesty's reign, chapter twenty-seven, in amendment thereof, the Act passed in the session held in the thirty-third year of Her Majesty's reign, chapter twelve, intituled " *An Act to remove certain restrictions with respect to the issue of bank notes in Nova Scotia*," the Act passed in the session held in the fiftieth and fifty-first years of Her Majesty's reign, chapter forty-seven, intituled " *An Act respecting the defacing of counterfeit notes, and the use of imitations of notes*," and chapter one hundred and twenty of the Revised Statutes of New Brunswick, " *Of Banking*," and the Act passed by the Legislature of the Province of New Brunswick in the nineteenth year of Her Majesty's reign, chapter forty-seven, intituled " *An Act to explain chapter 120, Title XXXI. of the Revised Statutes, 'Of Banking,'* " shall be repealed, except as to rights theretofore acquired or liabilities incurred in regard to any matter or thing done or contract or agreement made or entered into or offences commit'ed under the said chapters or Acts, and nothing in

Commencement of this Act.

Repeal of R. S. C., c 120 and of 51 V., c. 27 and 50-51 V., c. 47.

Saving clause.

this Act shall effect any action or proceedings then pending under the said chapter or Acts then repealed, but the same shall be decided as if such chapters and Acts had not been repealed.

SCHEDULE A.

BANKS WHOSE CHARTERS ARE CONTINUED BY THIS ACT.

1. The Bank of Montreal.
2. The Quebec Bank.
3. La Banque du Peuple.
4. The Molsons Bank.
5. The Bank of Toronto.
6. The Ontario Bank.
7. The Eastern Townships Bank.
8. La Banque Nationale.
9. La Banque Jacques Cartier.
10. The Merchants' Bank of Canada.
11. The Union Bank of Canada.
12. The Canadian Bank of Commerce.
13. The Dominion Bank.
14. The Merchants' Bank of Halifax.
15. The Bank of Nova Scotia.
16. The Bank of Yarmouth.
17. La Banque Ville Marie.
18. The Standard Bank of Canada.
19. The Bank of Hamilton.
20. The Halifax Banking Company.
21. La Banque d'Hochelaga.
22. The Imperial Bank of Canada.
23. La Banque de St. Hyacinthe.
24. The Bank of Ottawa.
25. The Bank of New Brunswick.
26. The Exchange Bank of Yarmouth.

27. The Union Bank of Halifax.
28. The People's Bank of Halifax.
29. La Banque de St. Jean.
30. The Commercial Bank of Windsor.
31. The Western Bank of Canada.
32. The Commercial Bank of Manitoba.
33. The Traders' Bank of Canada.
34. The People's Bank of New Brunswick.
35. The St. Stephen's Bank.
36. The Summerside Bank.

———

SCHEDULE B.

FORM OF ACT OF INCORPORATION OF NEW BANKS.

An Act to incorporate the   Bank.

Whereas the persons hereinafter named have, by their petition, prayed that an Act be passed for the purpose of establishing a bank in   , and it is expedient to grant the prayer of the said petition :

Therefore Her Majesty, by and with the advice and consent of the Senate and House of Commons of Canada, enacts as follows :—

1. The persons hereinafter named, together with such others as become shareholders in the corporation by this Act created, are hereby constituted a corporation by the name of   , hereinafter called " the Bank."

2. The capital stock of the bank shall be dollars.

3. The chief office of the bank shall be at

4.   shall be the provisional directors of the bank.

5. This Act shall, subject to the provisions of section sixteen of "The Bank Act," remain in force until the first day of July, in the year one thousand nine hundred and one.

SCHEDULE C.

FORM OF SECURITY UNDER SECTION SEVENTY-FOUR.

In consideration of an advance of   dollars, made by the (*name of bank*) to A. B., for which the said bank holds the following bills or notes (*describe fully the bills or notes held if any*), the goods, wares and merchandise mentioned below are hereby assigned to the said bank as security for the payment, on or before the   day of of the said advance, together with interest thereon at the rate of   per cent per annum from the day of   (*or*, of the said bills and notes, or renewals thereof, or substitutions therefor, and interest thereon, *or as the case may be.*)

This security is given under the provisions of section seventy-four of "The Bank Act," and is subject to all the provisions of the said Act.

The said goods, wares and merchandise are now owned by   and are now in   possession, and are free from any mortgage, lien or charge thereon, (*or as the case may be*), and are in (*place or places where goods are*), and are the following. (*particular description of goods assigned*).

Dated at   18   .

SCHEDULE D.

Return of the liabilities and assets of the   bank on the   day of   , A.D.

Capital authorized.................$

Capital subscribed.. $

Capital paid up.... ....$

Amount of rest or reserve fund.......$

Rate per cent of last dividend declared.   per cent.

LIABILITIES.

1. Notes in circulation.............$
2. Balance due to Dominion Govern-

ment, after deducting advances
for credits, pay-lists, &c........

3. Balance due to Provincial Governments ....

4. Deposits by the public, payable on
demand........ ....

5. Deposits by the public, payable after
notice or on a fixed day........

6. Loans from other banks in Canada,
secured .. ..

7. Deposits, payable on demand or
after notice or on a fixed day,
made by other banks in Canada.

8. Balances due to other banks in
Canada in daily exchanges......

9. Balances due to agencies of the
bank, or to other banks or agencies in foreign countries........

10. Balances due to agencies of the
bank, or to other banks or agencies in the United Kingdom....

11. Liabilities not included under foregoing heads.............. ..

$ _____

ASSETS.

1. Specie ....$

2. Dominion notes ....

3. Deposits with Dominion Government for security of note circulation ....

4. Notes and cheques on other banks..

5 Loans to other banks in Canada,
secured ....

6. Deposits, payable on demand or
after notice or on a fixed day,
made with other banks in Canada.

7. Balances due from other banks in Canada in daily exchanges......

8. Balances due from agencies of the bank, or from other banks or agencies in foreign countries ...

9. Balances due from agencies of the bank, or from other banks or agencies in the United Kingdom.

10. Dominion Government debentures or stocks ....

11. Canadian municipal securities, and British, Provincial, or foreign, or colonial public securities, (other than Dominion) ....

12. Canadian, British and other railway securities................

13. Call loans on bonds and stocks.....

14. Current loans................ ....

15. Loans to the Government of Canada

16. Loans to Provincial Governments...

17. Overdue debts................ ......

18. Real estate, the property of the bank (other than the bank premises)...

19. Mortgages on real estate sold by the bank.....................

20. Bank premises................ ....

21. Other assets not included under the foregoing heads..............

$ _____

Aggregate amount of loans to directors, and firms of which they are partners, $

Average amount of specie held during the month, $

Average amount of Dominion Notes held during the month, $

Greatest amount of notes in circulation at any time during the month, $

I declare that the above return has been prepared under my direction and is correct according to the books of the bank.

E. F.,

Chief Accountant.

We declare that the foregoing return is made up from the books of the bank, and that to the best of our knowledge and belief it is correct, and shows truly and clearly the financial position of the bank ; and we further declare that the bank has never, at any time during the period to which the said return relates, held less than forty per cent of its cash reserves in Dominion notes.

(*Place*)   this   day of

A. B., *President.*
C. D., *General Manager.*

EXTRACTS FROM "THE CRIMINAL CODE OF 1892" WHICH
COMES INTO FORCE ON

The 1st Day of July, 1893,

AND WHICH ARE OF SPECIAL IMPORTANCE TO BANKS AND
BANKERS.

AN ACT RESPECTING THE CRIMINAL LAW.

————

PRELIMINARY.

Short title.

1. This Act may be cited for all purposes as "The Criminal Code of 1892."

Commencement of Act.

2. This Act shall come into force on the first day of July, 1893.

Explanation of terms

3. In this Act the following expressions have the meanings assigned to them in this section unless the context requires otherwise.

(c.) The expression "Banker" includes any director of any incorporated bank or banking company; R.S.C., c. 164, s. 2 (g).

(g.) The expression "Document of title to goods" includes any bill of lading, India warrant, dock warrant, warehouse-keeper's certificate, warrant or order for the delivery or transfer of any goods or valuable thing, bought and sold note, or any other document used in the ordinary course of business as proof of the possession or control of goods, authorizing or purporting to authorize, either by indorsement or by delivery, the possessor of such document to transfer or receive any goods thereby represented or therein mentioned or referred to; R.S.C., c. 164, s. 2. (a).

(bb.) The expression "trustee" means a trustee on some express trust created by some deed, will or instrument in writing, or by parol, or otherwise, and includes the heir or personal representative of any such trustee, and every other person upon or to whom the duty of such trust has devolved or come, whether by appointment of a court or otherwise, and also an executor and administrator, and an official manager, assignee, liquidator or other like officer acting under any Act relating to joint stock companies, bankruptcy or insolvency, and any person who is, by the law of the Province of Quebec, an "*administrateur*" or "*fidécommissaire*"; and the expression "trust" includes whatever is by that law an "*administration*" or "*fidécommission*;' R.S.C., c. 164, s. 2 (*c*).

(*cc.*) The expression "valuable security" includes any order, exchequer acquittance or other security entitling or evidencing the title of any person to any share or interest in any public stock or fund, whether of Canada or of any Province thereof, or of the United Kingdom, or of Great Britain or Ireland, or any British colony or possession, or of any foreign state, or in any fund of any body corporate, company or society, whether within Canada or the United Kingdom, or any British colony or possession, or in any foreign state or country, or to any deposit in any savings' bank or other bank, and also includes any debenture, deed, bond, bill, note, warrant, order or other security for money or for payment of money, whether of Canada or of any Province thereof, or of the United Kingdom or of any British colony or possession, or of any foreign state, and any document of title to lands or goods as hereinbefore defined wheresoever such lands or goods are situate, and any stamp or writing which secures or evidences title to or interest in any chattel personal, or any release, receipt, discharge or other instrument, evidencing payment of money, or the delivery of any chattel personal; and every such valuable security shall, where value is material, be deemed to be of value equal to that of such unsatisfied money, chattel personal, share, interest or deposit, for the securing or payment of which, or delivery or transfer or sale of which, or for the entitling or evidencing title to which, such valuable security is applicable, or to that of such money or chattel personal, the payment or delivery of which is evidenced by such valuable security; 53 V., c. 37, s. 20.

Spreading false news.

126. Every one is guilty of an indictable offence and liable to one year's imprisonment who wilfully and knowingly publishes any false news or tale whereby injury or mischief is or is likely to be occasioned to any public interest.

Gaming in stocks and merchandise

201. Every one is guilty of an indictable offence and liable to five years' imprisonment, and to a fine of five hundred dollars, who, with the intent to make gain or profit by the rise or fall in price of any stock of any incorporated or unincorporated company or undertaking, either in Canada or elsewhere, or of any goods, wares or merchandise, —

(a.) without the *bona fide* intention of acquiring any such shares, goods, wares or merchandise, or of selling the same, as the case may be, makes or signs, or authorises to be made or signed, any contract or agreement, oral or written, purporting to be for the sale or purchase of any such shares of stock, goods, wares or merchandise ; or

(b.) makes or signs, or authorizes to be made or signed, any contract or agreement, oral or written, purporting to be for the sale or purchase of any such shares of stock, goods, wares or merchandise in respect of which no delivery of the thing sold or purchased is made or received, and without the *bona fide* intention to make or receive such delivery.

2. But it is not an offence if the broker of the purchaser receives delivery, on his behalf, of the article sold, notwithstanding that such broker retains or pledges the same as security for the advance of the purchase money or any part thereof.

3. Every office or place of business wherein is carried on the business of making or signing, or procuring to be made or signed, or negotiating or bargaining for the making or signing of such contracts of sale or purchase as are prohibited in this section is a common gaming house, and every one who as principal or agent occupies, uses, manages or maintains the same is the keeper of a common gaming house. 51 V., c. 42, ss. 1 & 3.

Theft defined.

305. Theft or stealing is the act of fraudulently and without colour of right taking, or fraudulently and without colour

of right converting to the use of any person, anything capable of being stolen, with intent—

(*a*) to deprive the owner, or any person having any special property or interest therein, temporarily or absolutely of such thing or of such property or interest ; or

(*b*) to pledge the same or deposit it as security ; or

(*c*) to part with it under a condition as to its return which the person parting with it may be unable to perform ; or

(*d*) to deal with it in such a manner that it cannot be restored in the condition in which it was at the time of such taking and conversion.

2. The taking or conversion may be fraudulent, although effected without secrecy or attempt at concealment.

3. It is immaterial whether the thing converted was taken for the purpose of conversion, or whether it was, at the time of the conversion, in the lawful possession of the person converting. .

4. Theft is committed when the offender moves the thing or causes it to move or to be moved, or begins to cause it to become moveable, with intent to steal it.

5. Provided, that no factor or agent shall be guilty of theft by pledging or giving a lien on any goods or document of title to goods intrusted to him for the purpose of sale or otherwise, for any sum of money not greater than the amount due to him from his principal at the time of pledging or giving a lien on the same, together with the amount of any bill of exchange accepted by him for or on account of his principal.

6. Provided, that if any servant, contrary to the orders of his master, takes from his possession any food for the purpose of giving the same or having the same given to any horse or other animal belonging to or in the possession of his master, the servant so offending shall not, by reason thereof, be guilty of theft.   R.S.C., c. 164, s. 63.

309. Every one commits theft who, being entrusted, either solely or jointly with any other person, with any power of attorney for the sale, mortgage, pledge or other disposition of any property, real or personal, whether capable of being *Theft by person holding a power of attorney.*

stolen or not, fraudulently sells, mortgages, pledges or otherwise disposes of the same or any part thereof, or fraudulently converts the proceeds of any sale, mortgage, pledge or other disposition of such property, or any part of such proceeds, to some purpose other than that for which he was intrusted with such power of attorney.   R.S.C., c. 164, s. 62.

Theft by misappropriating proceeds held under direction.

310. Every one commits theft who, having received, either solely or jointly with any other person, any money or valuable security or any power of attorney for the sale of any property, real or personal, with a direction that such money, or any part thereof, or the proceeds, or any part of the proceeds of such security, or such property, shall be applied to any purpose or paid to any person specified in such direction, in violation of good faith and contrary to such direction, fraudulently applies to any other purpose or pays to any other person such money or proceeds, or any part thereof.

2. Provided, that where the person receiving such money, security or power of attorney, and the person from whom he receives it, deal with each other on such terms that all money paid to the former would, in the absence of any such direction, be properly treated as an item in a debtor and creditor account between them, this section shall not apply unless such direction is in writing.

Clerks and servants

319. Every one is guilty of an indictable offence and liable to fourteen years' imprisonment who,

(a.) being a clerk or servant, or being employed for the purpose or in the capacity of a clerk or servant, steals anything belonging to or in the possession of his master or employer ; or

(b.) being a cashier, assistant cashier, manager, officer, clerk or servant of any bank, or savings bank, steals any bond, obligation, bill obligatory or of credit, or other bill or note, or any security for money, or any money or effects of such bank or lodged or deposited with any such bank ;

(c.) being employed in the service of Her Majesty, or of the Government of Canada or the Government of any province of Canada, or of any municipality, steals anything in his possession by virtue of his employment.   R.S.C., c. 164, ss. 51, 52, 53, 54 and 59.

320. Every one is guilty of an indictable offence and liable to fourteen years' imprisonment who steals anything by any act or omission amounting to theft under the provisions of sections 308, 309 and 310.   *Agents and attorneys.*

363. Every one is guilty of an indictable offence and liable to seven years' imprisonment who, being a trustee of any property for the use or benefit, either in whole or in part, of some other person, or for any public or charitable purpose, with intent to defraud, and in violation of his trust, converts anything of which he is trustee to any use not authorized by the trust.   *Criminal breach of trust.*

547 No proceeding or prosecution against a trustee for a criminal breach of trust, as defined in section 363, shall be commenced without the sanction of the Attorney General. R.S.C., c. 164, s. 65.   *Trustee fraudulently disposing of money.*

364. Every one is guilty of an indictable offence and liable to seven years' imprisonment who, being a director, manager, public officer or member of any body corporate or public company, with intent to defraud—   *False accounting by official.*

(*a.*) destroys, alters, mutilates or falsifies any book, paper, writing or valuable security belonging to the body corporate or public company ; or

(*b.*) makes, or concurs in making, any false entry, or omits or concurs in omitting to enter any material particular, in any book of account or other document.   R.S.C., c. 164, s. 68.

365. Every one is guilty of an indictable offence and liable to five years' imprisonment who, being a promoter, director, public officer or manager of any body corporate or public company, either existing or intended to be formed, makes, circulates or publishes, or concurs in making, circulating or publishing, any prospectus, statement or account which he knows to be false in any material particular, with intent to induce persons (whether ascertained or not) to become shareholders or partners, or with intent to deceive or defraud the members, shareholders or creditors, or any of them   *False statement by official*

(whether ascertained or not) of such body corporate or public company, or with intent to induce any person to entrust or advance any property to such body corporate or public company, or to enter into any security for the benefit thereof. R.S.C., c. 164, s. 69.

False accounting by clerk. 366. Every one is guilty of an indictable offence and liable to seven years' imprisonment who, being or acting in the capacity of an officer, clerk or servant, with intent to defraud—

(*a.*) destroys, alters, mutilates or falsifies any book, paper writing, valuable security or document which belongs to or is in the possession of his employer, or has been received by him for or on behalf of his employer, or concurs in so doing ; or

(*b*) makes, or concurs in making, any false entry in, or omits or alters, or concurs in omitting or altering, any material particular from, any such book, paper writing, valuable security or document.

Warehousemen, etc., giving false receipts ; knowingly using the same. 376 Every one is guilty of an indictable offence and liable to three years' imprisonment who,—

(*a.*) being the keeper of any warehouse, or a forwarder, miller, master of a vessel, wharfinger, keeper of a cove, yard, harbour or other place for storing timber, deals, staves, boards, or lumber, curer or packer of pork, or dealer in wood, carrier, factor, agent or other person, or a clerk or other person in his employ, knowingly and wilfully gives to any person a writing purporting to be a receipt for, or an acknowledgement of, any goods or other property as having been received into his warehouse, vessel, cove, wharf, or other place, or in any such place about which he is employed, or in any other manner received by him, or by the person in or about whose business he is employed before the goods or other property named in such receipt, acknowledgment or writing have been actually delivered to or received by him as aforesaid, with intent to mislead, deceive, injure or defraud any person, although such person is then unknown to him ; or

(*b.*) knowingly and wilfully accepts, transmits or uses any such false receipt or acknowledgment or writing. R.S.C., c. 164, s 73.

377. Every one is guilty of an indictable offence and liable to three years' imprisonment, who—

(*a.*) having, in his name, shipped or delivered to the keeper of any warehouse, or to any other factor, agent or carrier, to be shipped or carried, any merchandise upon which the consignee has advanced any money or given any valuable security afterwards, with intent to deceive, defraud or injure such consignee, in violation of good faith, and without the consent of such consignee, makes any disposition of such merchandise different from and inconsistent with the agreement made in that behalf between him and such consignee at the time of or before such money was so advanced or such negotiable security so given ; or

(*b.*) knowingly and wilfully aids and assists in making such disposition for the purpose of deceiving, defrauding or injuring such consignee.

2. No person commits an offence under this section who, before making such disposition of such merchandise, pays or tenders to the consignee the full amount of any advance made thereon. R.S.C., c. 164, s. 74.

Owners of merchandise disposing thereof contrary to agreements with consignees who have made advances thereon.

378. Every person is guilty of an indictable offence and liable to three years' imprisonment who, —

(*a.*) wilfully makes any false statement in any receipt, certificate or acknowledgment for grain, timber or other goods or property which can be used for any of the purposes mentioned in *The Bank Act ;* or

(*b*) having given, or after any clerk or person in his employ has, to his knowledge, given, as having been received by him in any mill, warehouse, vessel, cove or other place, any such receipt, certificate or acknowledgment for any such grain, timber or other goods or property,—or having obtained any such receipt, certificate or acknowledgment, and after having endorsed or assigned it to any bank or person, afterwards, and without the consent of the holder or endorsee in writing, or the production and delivery of the receipt, certificate or acknowledgment, wilfully alienates or

Making false statements in receipts for property that can be used under " The Bank Act : " fraudulently dealing with property to which such receipt refer.

parts with, or does not deliver to such holder or owner of such receipt, certificate or acknowledgment, the grain, timber, goods or other property therein mentioned.   R.S.C., c. 164, s. 75.

Innocent partners.

379. If any offence mentioned in any of the three sections next preceding is committed by the doing of anything in the name of any firm, company or co-partnership of persons the person by whom such thing is actually done, or who connives at the doing thereof, is guilty of the offence, and not any other person.   R.S.C., c. 164, s. 76.

Conspiracy to defraud.

394. Every one is guilty of an indictable offence and liable to seven years' imprisonment who conspires with any other person, by deceit or falsehood or other fraudulent means, to defraud the public or any person, ascertained or unascertained, or to affect the public market price of stocks, shares, merchandise or anything else publicly sold, whether such deceit or falsehood or other fraudulent means would or would not amount to a false pretense as hereinbefore defined.

FORGERY.

Document defined.

419. A document means in this part any paper, parchment, or other material used for writing or printing, marked with matter capable of being read, but does not include trade marks on articles of commerce, or inscriptions on stone or metal or other like material.

"Bank note" and "exchequer bill", defined.

420. "Bank note" includes all negotiable instruments issued by or on behalf of any person, body corporate, or company carrying on the business of banking in any part of the world, or,issued by the authority of the Parliament of Canada or of any foreign prince, or state, or government, or any governor or other authority lawfully authorized thereto in any of Her Majesty's dominions, and intended to be used as equivalent to money, either immediately upon their issue or at some time subsequent thereto, and all bank bills and bank post bills ;

(a) "Exchequer bill" includes Exchequer bonds, notes, de

bentures and other securities issued under the authority of the Parliament of Canada, or under the authority of any Legislature of any Province forming part of Canada, whether before or after such Province so became a part of Canada.

421. The expression " false document " means —

(*a*) a document the whole or some material part of which False document defined. purports to be made by or on behalf of any person who did not make or authorize the making thereof, or which, though made by, or by the authority of, the person who purports to make it is falsely dated as to time or place of making, where either is material; or

(*b*) a document the whole or some material part of which. purports to be made by or on behalf of some person who did not in fact exist; or

(*c*) a document which is made in the name of an existing person, either by that person or by his authority, with the fraudulent intention that the document should pass as being made by some person, real or fictitious, other than the person who makes or authorizes it.

2. It is not necessary that the fraudulent intention should appear on the face of the document, but it may be proved by external evidence.

422. Forgery is the making of a false document, knowing it to be false, with the intention that it shall in any way be Forgery defined. used or acted upon as genuine, to the prejudice of any one whether within Canada or not, or that some person should be induced, by the belief that it is genuine, to do or refrain from doing anything, whether within Canada or not.

2. Making a false document includes altering a genuine document in any material part, and making any material addition to it or adding to it any false date, attestation, seal or other thing which is material, or by making any material alteration in it, either by erasure, obliteration, removal or otherwise.

3. Forgery is complete as soon as the document is made with such knowledge and intent as aforesaid, though the offender may not have intended that any particular person should use or act upon it as genuine, or be induced, by the

belief that it is genuine, to do or refrain from doing anything.

4. Forgery is complete although the false document may be incomplete, or may not purport to be such a document as would be binding in law, if it be so made as, and is such as to indicate that it was intended, to be acted on as genuine.

423. Every one who commits forgery of the documents hereinafter mentioned is guilty of an indictable offence and liable to the following punishment :—

(*A.*) to imprisonment for life if the document forged purports to be, or was intended by the offender to be understood to be or to be used as—

(*p.*) any entry in any book or register, or any certificate, coupon, share, warrant or other document which by any law or any recognized practice is evidence of the title of any person to any such stock, interest or share, or to any dividend or interest payable in respect thereof ; R.S.C., c. 165, s. 11 ; or

(*r*) any bank note or bill of exchange, promissory note or cheque, or any acceptance, endorsement or assignment thereof ; R.S.C., c. 165, ss. 18, 25 and 28 ; or

(*u.*) any deed, bond, debenture, or writing obligatory, or any warrant, order, or other security for money or payment of money, whether negotiable or not, or endorsement or assignment thereof ; R.S.C., c. 165, ss. 26 and 32 ; or

(*v.*) any accountable receipt or acknowledgement of the deposit, receipt, or delivery of money or goods, or endorsement or assignment thereof ; R.S.C., c. 165, s. 29 ; or

(*w.*) any bill of lading, charter-party, policy of insurance, or any shipping document accompanying a bill of lading, or any endorsement or assignment thereof ; or

(*x.*) any warehouse receipt, dock warrant, dock-keeper's certificate, delivery order, or warrant for the delivery of goods, or of any valuable thing, or any endorsement or assignment thereof ; or

(*y.*) any other document used in the ordinary course of business as proof of the possession or control of goods, or as authorizing, either on endorsement or delivery, the possessor of such document to transfer or receive any goods.

424. Every one is guilty of an indictable offence who, knowing a document to be forged, uses, deals with, or acts upon it, or attempts to use, deal with, or act upon it, or causes or attempts to cause any person to use, deal with, or act upon it, as if it were genuine, and is liable to the same punishment as if he had forged the document. · *Uttering forged documents.*

2. It is immaterial where the document was forged.

428. Every one is guilty of an indictable offence who, with intent to defraud, causes or procures any telegram to be sent or delivered as being sent by the authority of any person, knowing that it is not sent by such authority, with intent that such telegram should be acted on as being sent by that person's authority, and is liable, upon conviction thereof, to the same punishment as if he had forged a document to the same effect as that of the telegram. *Sending telegrams in false names.*

429. Every one is guilty of an indictable offence and liable to two years' imprisonment who, with intent to injure or alarm any person, sends, causes, or procures to be sent, any telegram or letter or other message containing matter which he knows to be false. *Sending false telegrams.*

430. Every one is guilty of an indictable offence and liable to fourteen years' imprisoment who, without lawful athority or excuse (the proof whereof shall lie on him), purchases or receives from any person, or has in his custody or possession, any forged bank note, or forged blank bank note, whether complete or not, knowing it to be forged. R.S.C., c. 165, s. 19. · *Possessing forged bank notes.*

431. Every one is guilty of an indictable offence who, with intent to defraud and without lawful authority or excuse, makes or executes, draws, signs, accepts or indorses, in the name or on the account of another person, by procuration or otherwise, any document, or makes use of or utters any such document knowing it to be so made, executed, signed, accepted or endorsed, and is liable to the same punishment as if he had forged such document. R.S.C., c. 165, s. 30. *Drawing document without authority.*

434. Every one is guilty of an indictable offence and liable to fourteen years' imprisonment who, without lawful authority or excuse (the proof whereof shall lie on him)— *Instruments of forgery.*

(a) makes, begins to make, uses or knowingly has in his possession, any machinery or instrument or material for making Exchequer bill paper, revenue paper or paper intended to resemble the bill paper of any firm or body corporate, or person carrying on the business of banking ; R.S.C., c. 165, ss. 14, 16, 20 & 24 ; or

(b) engraves or makes upon any plate or material anything purporting to be, or apparently intended to resemble, the whole or any part of any Exchequer bill or bank note ; R.S.C., c. 165, ss. 20, 22 & 24 ; or

(c) uses any such plate or material for printing any part of any such Exchequer bill or bank note ; R.S.C., c. 165, ss. 22 & 23 ; or

(d) knowingly has in his possession any such plate or material as aforesaid ; R.S.C., c. 165, ss. 22 & 23 ; or

(e) makes, uses or knowingly has in his possession any Exchequer bill paper, revenue paper, or any paper intended to resemble any bill paper of any firm, body corporate, company, or person, carrying on the business of banking, or any paper upon which is written or printed the whole or any part of an Exchequer bill, or of any bank note ; R. S.C., c. 165, ss. 15, 16, 20 & 24 ; or

(f) engraves or makes upon any plate or material anything intended to resemble the whole or any distinguishing part of any bond or undertaking for the payment of money used by any dominion, colony or possession of Her Majesty, or by any foreign prince or state, or by any body corporate, or other body of the like nature, whether within Her Majesty's dominions or without ; R.S.C., c. 165, s. 25 ; or

(g) uses any such plate or other material for printing the whole or any part of such bond or undertaking ; R.S.C., c. 165, s 25 ; or

(h) knowingly offers, disposes of or has in his possession any paper upon which such bond or undertaking, or any part thereof, has been printed.   R.S.C., c. 165, s. 25.

Making false entries in books relating to public funds.   440. Every one is guilty of an indictable offence and liable to fourteen years' imprisonment who, with intent to defraud,—

(*a*.) makes an untrue entry or any alteration in any book of account kept by the Government of Canada, or of any Province of Canada, or by any bank for any such Government, in which books are kept the accounts of the owners of any stock, annuity or other public fund transferable for the time being in any such books, or who, in any matter, wilfully falsifies any of the said books ; or

(*b*.) makes any transfer of any share or interest of or in any stock, annuity or public fund, transferable for the time being at any of the said banks, in the name of any person other than the owner of such share or interest.   R.S.C., c. 165, s. 11.

441. Every one is guilty of an indictable offence and liable to seven years' imprisonment who, being in the employment of the Government of Canada, or of any Province of Canada, or of any bank in which any books of account mentioned in the last preceding section are kept, with intent to defraud, makes out or delivers any dividend warrant, or any warrant for the payment of any annuity, interest or money payable at any of the said banks, for an amount greater or less than that to which the person on whose account such warrant is made out is entitled.   R.S.C., c. 165, s. 12. *Clerks issuing false dividend warrants.*

442. Every one is guilty of an offence and liable, on summary conviction before two justices of the peace, to a fine of one hundred dollars or three months' imprisonment, or both, who designs, engraves, prints or in any manner makes, executes, utters, issues, distributes, circulates or uses any business or professional card, notice, placard, circular, handbill or advertisement in the likeness or similitude of any bank note, or any obligation or security of any Government or any bank.   50 and 51 V., c. 47, s. 2, ; 53 V., c. 31, s. 3. *Printing circulars, etc., in likeness of notes.*

458. Every one is guilty of an indictable offence and liable to fourteen years' imprisonment who falsely and deceitfully personates— *Personation of certain persons.*

(*a*.) any owner of any share or interest of or in any stock, annuity, or other public fund transferable in any book of account kept by the Government of Canada or of any Province thereof, or by any bank for any such Government; or

(*b.*) any owner of any share or interest of or in the debt of any public body, or of or in the debt or capital stock of any body corporate, company, or society; or

(*c.*) any owner of any dividend, coupon, certificate or money payable in respect of any such share or interest as aforesaid; or

(*d.*) any owner of any share or interest in any claim for a grant of land from the Crown, or for any scrip or other payment or allowance in lieu of such grant of land; or

(*e.*) any person duly authorised by any power of attorney to transfer any such share, or interest, or to receive any dividend, coupon, certificate or money, on behalf of the person entitled thereto—

and thereby transfers or endeavours to transfer any share or interest belonging to such owner, or thereby obtains or endeavours to obtain, as if he were the true and lawful owner or were the person so authorized by such power of attorney, any money due to any such owner or payable to the person so authorized, or any certificate, coupon, or share warrant, grant of land, or scrip, or allowance in lieu thereof, or other document which, by any law in force, or any usage existing at the time, is deliverable to the owner of any such stock or fund, or to the person authorized by any such power of attorney.   R.S.C., c. 165, s. 9.

INDEX.